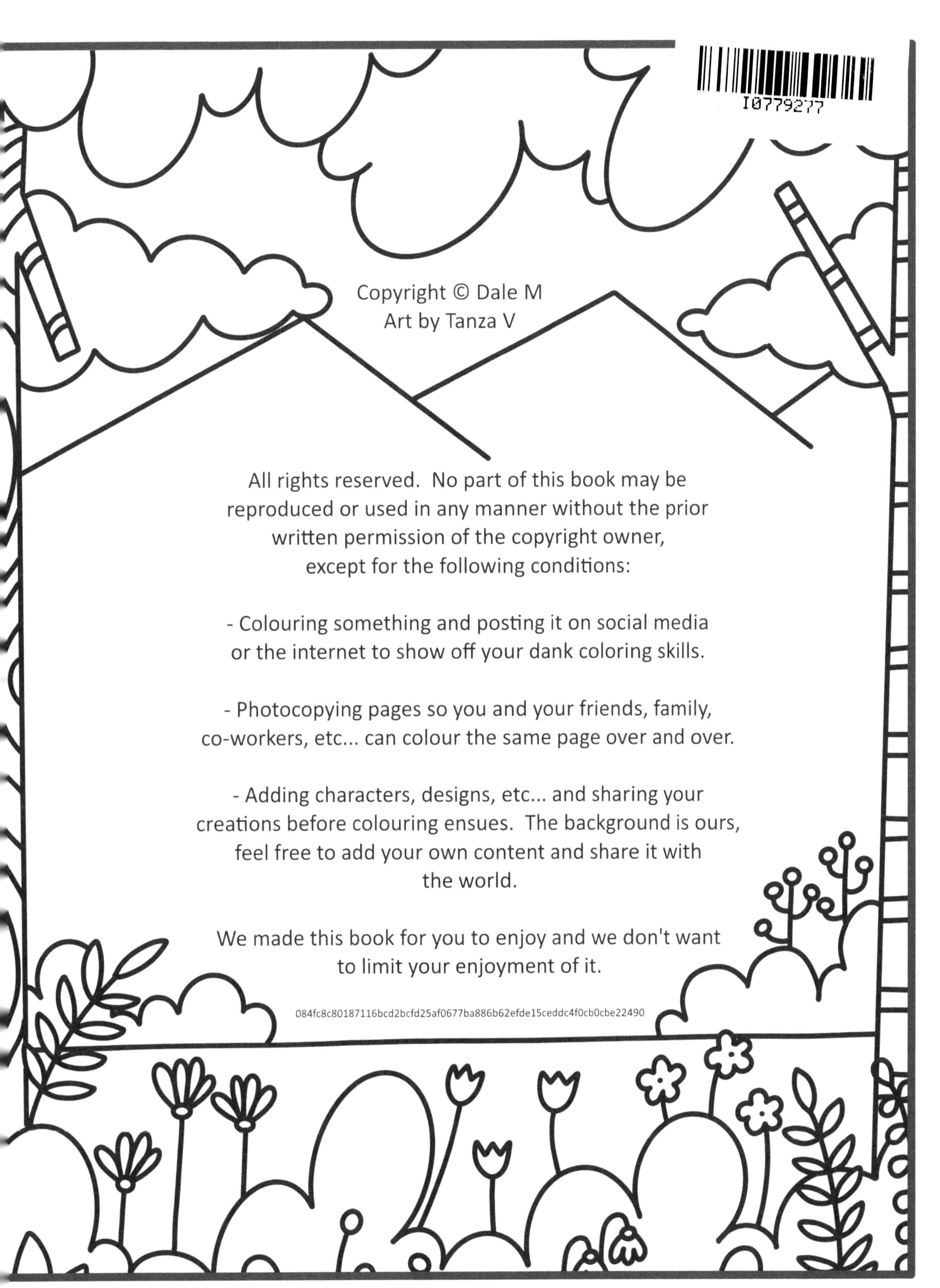

Copyright © Dale M
Art by Tanza V

084fc8c80187116bcd2bcfd25af0677ba886b62efde15ceddc4f0cb0cbe22490

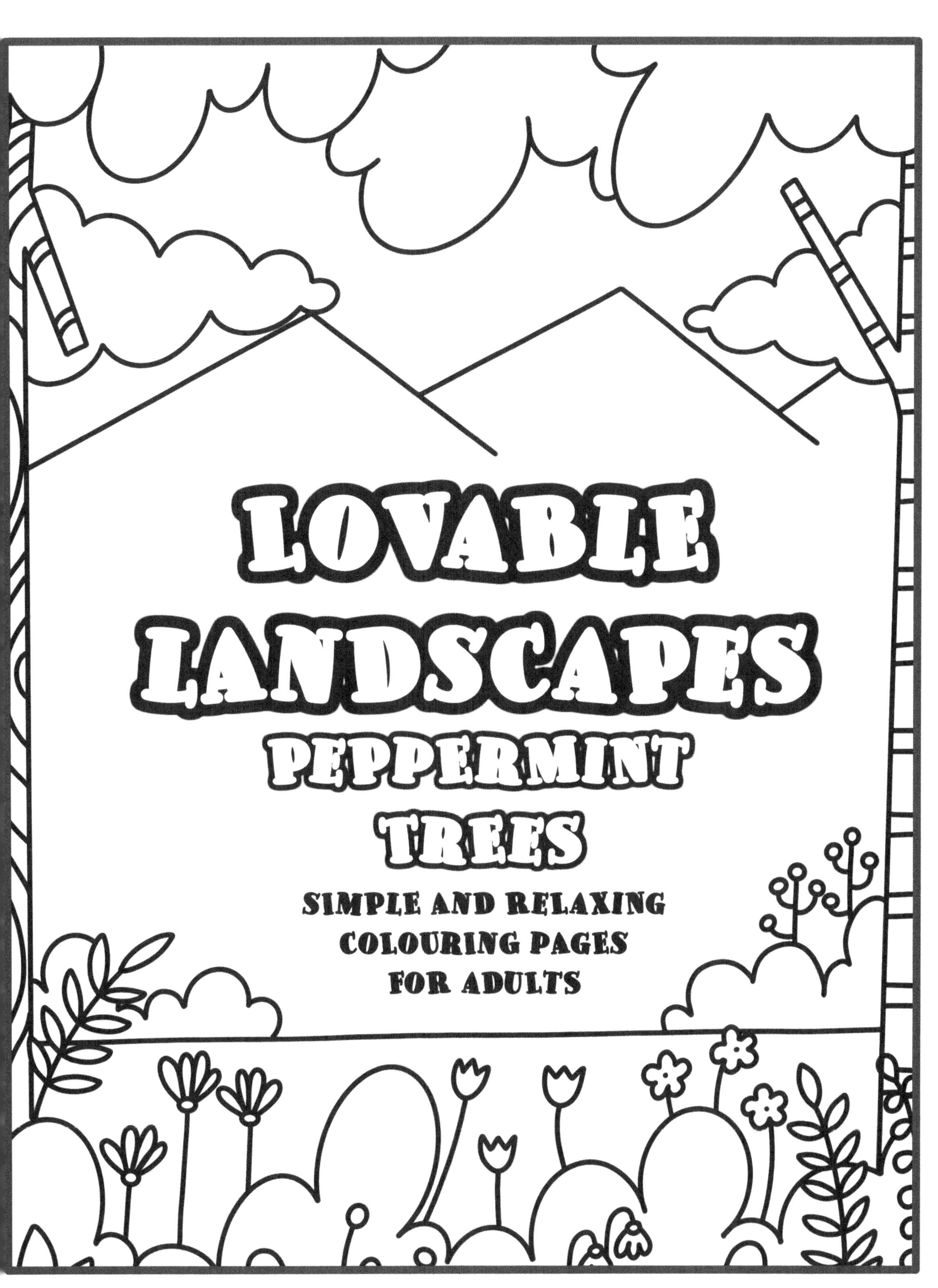

LOVABLE
LANDSCAPES
PEPPERMINT
TREES
SIMPLE AND RELAXING
COLOURING PAGES
FOR ADULTS

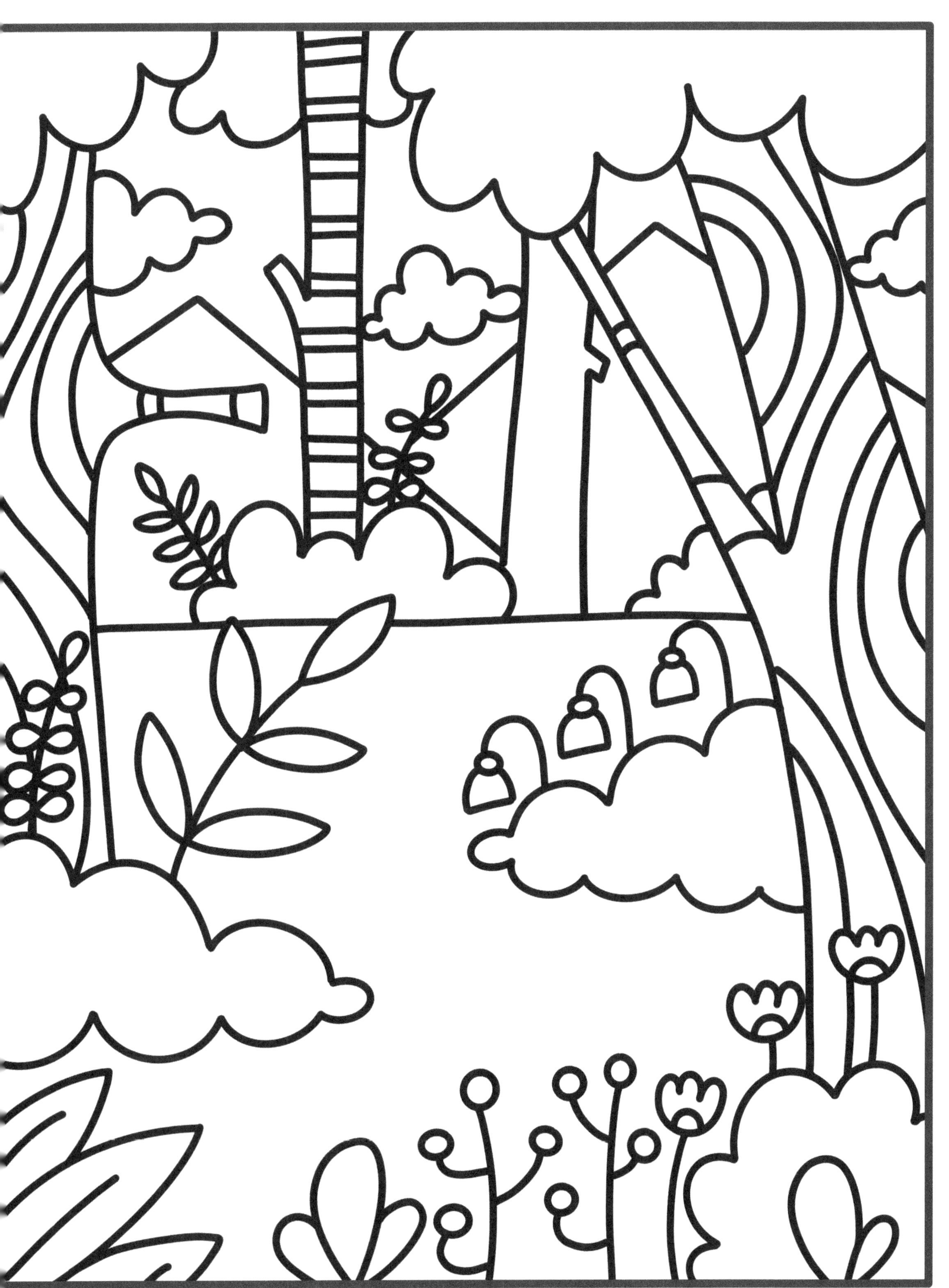

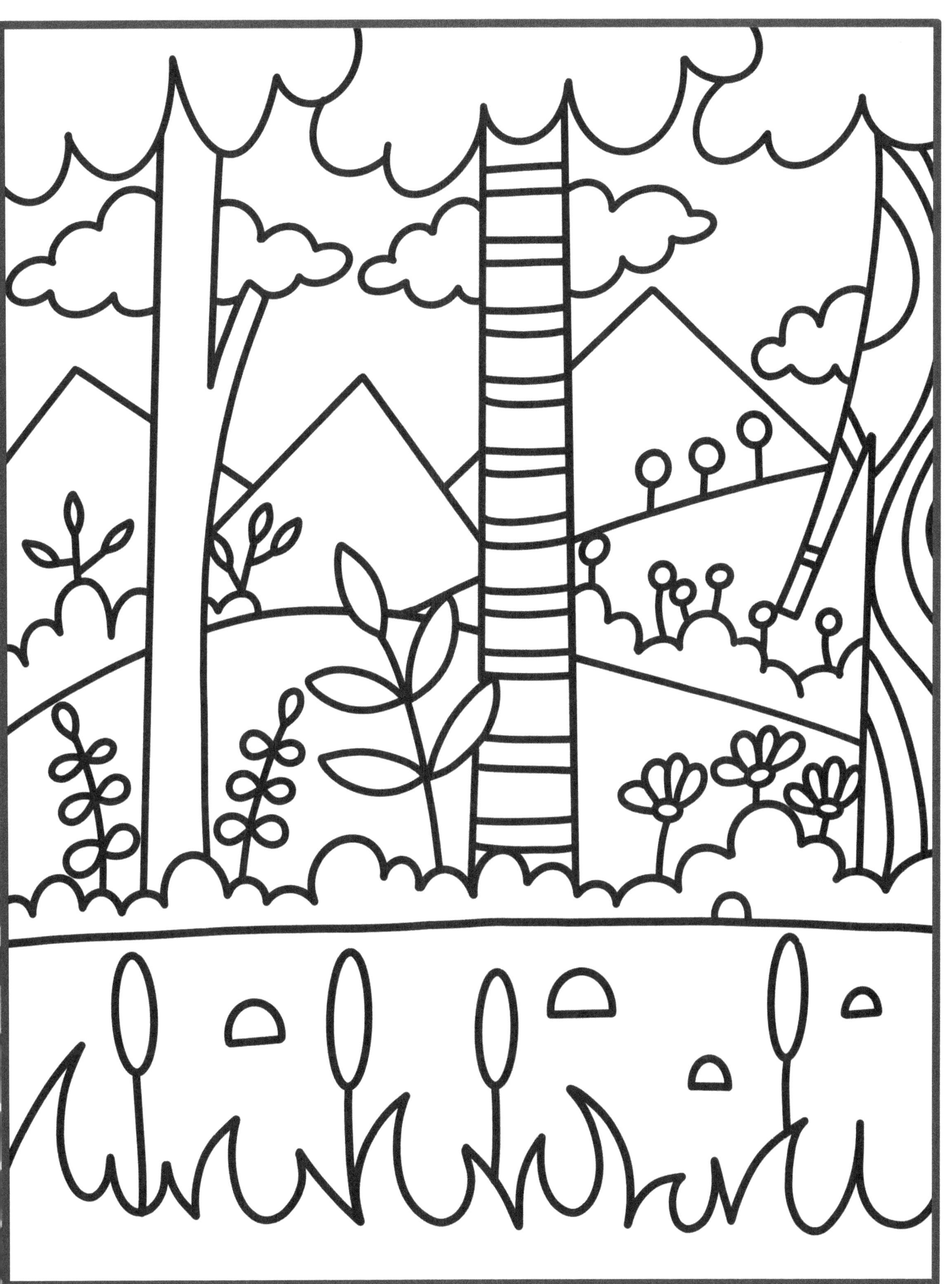

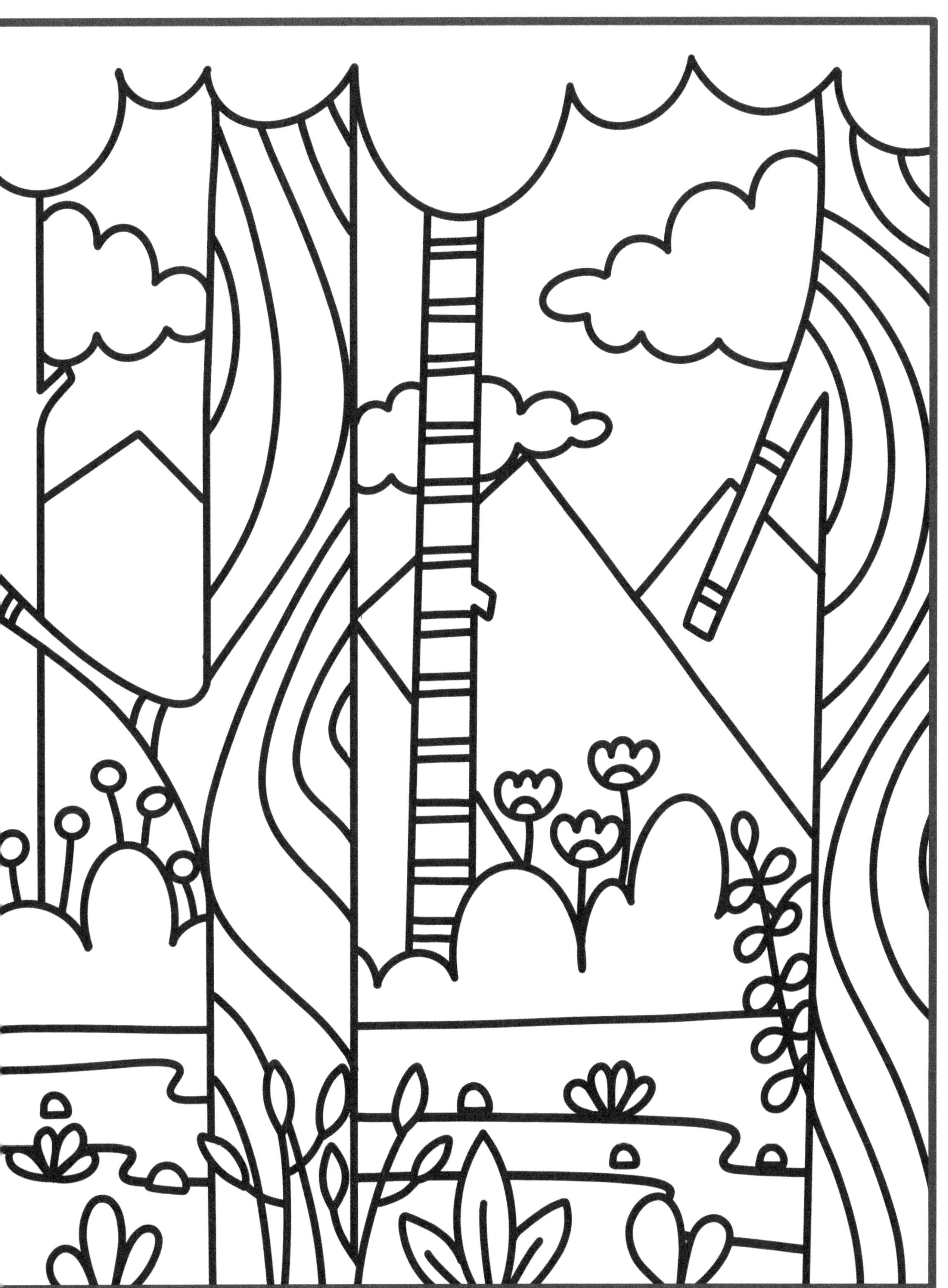

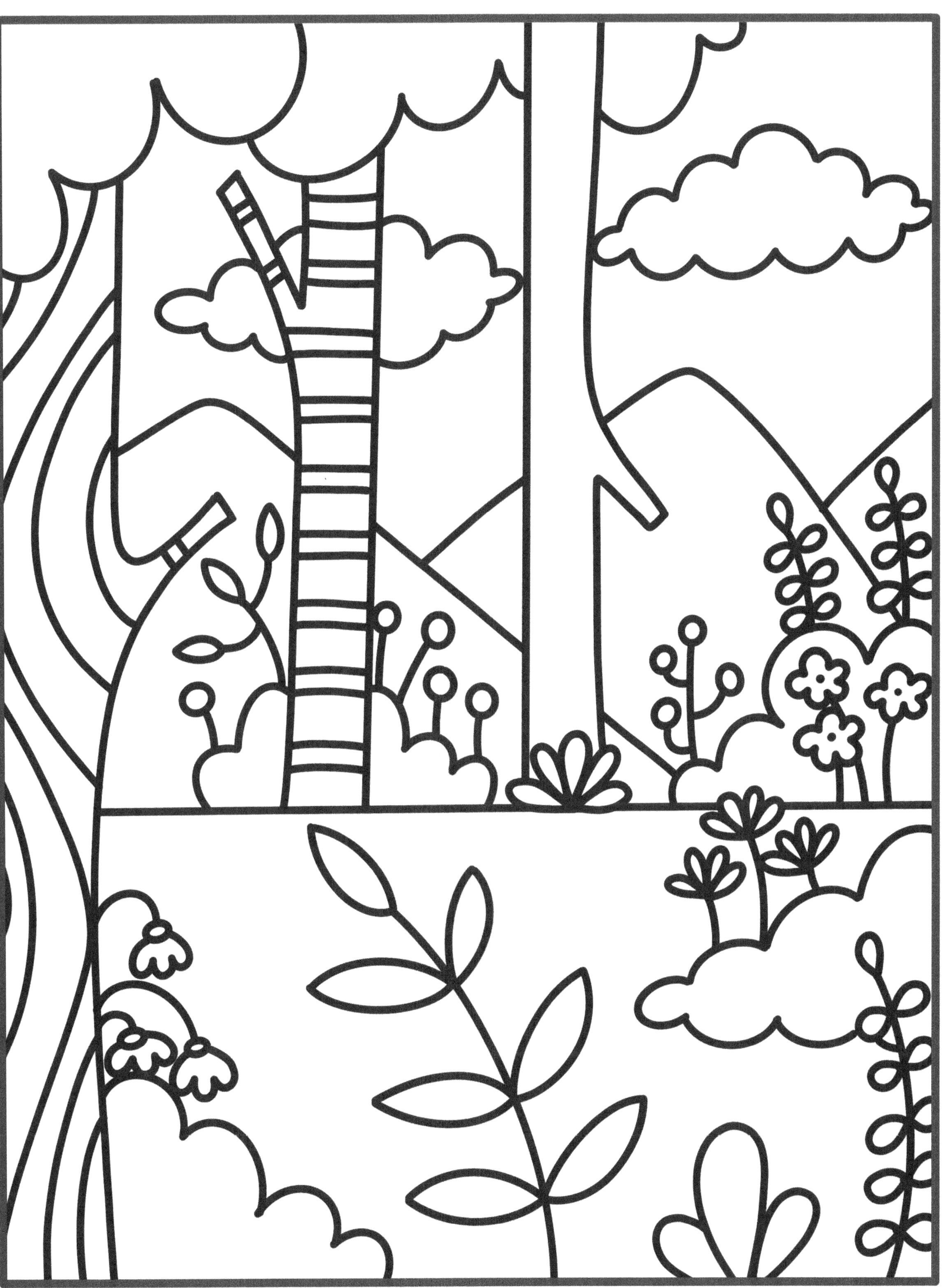

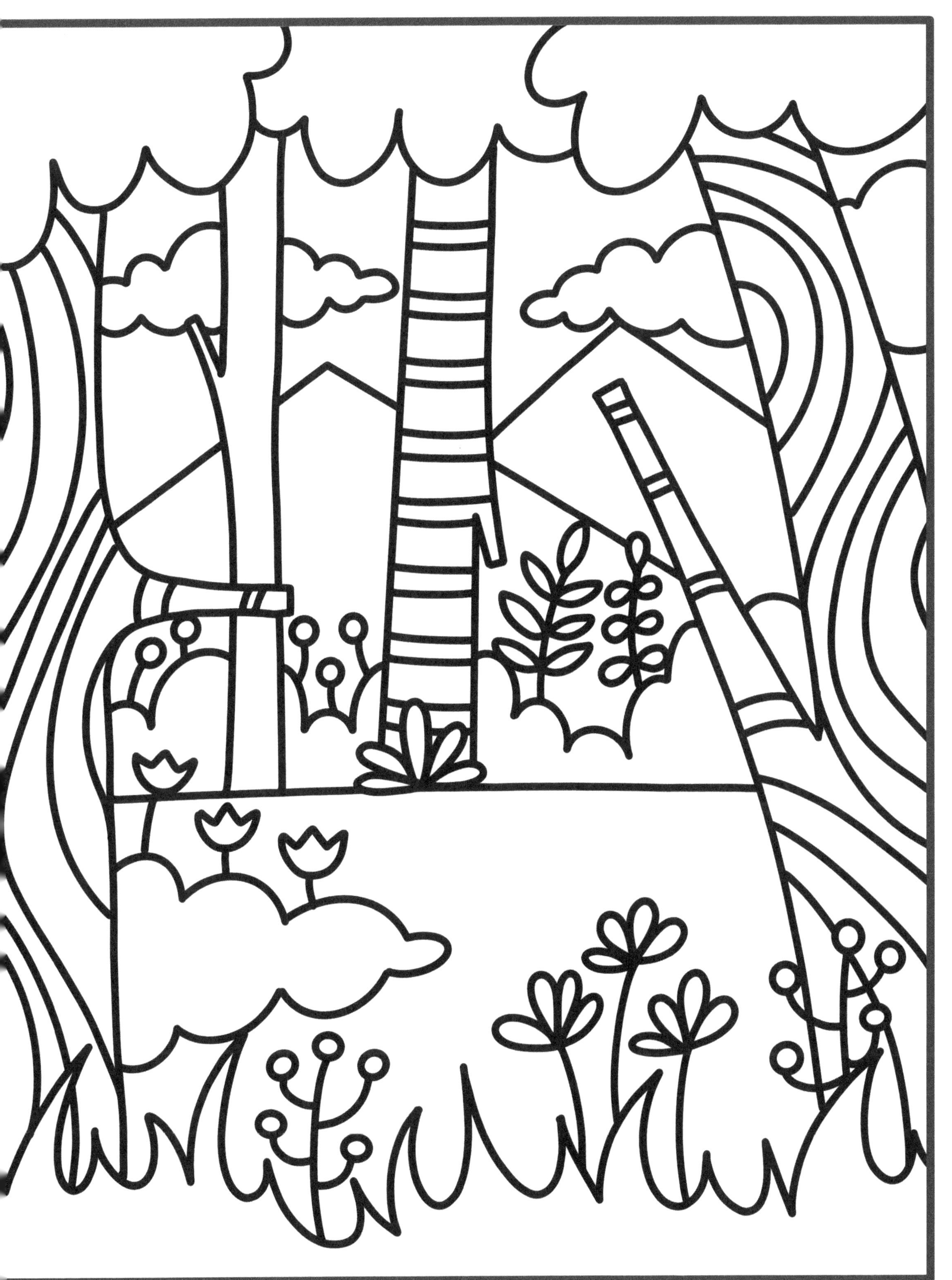

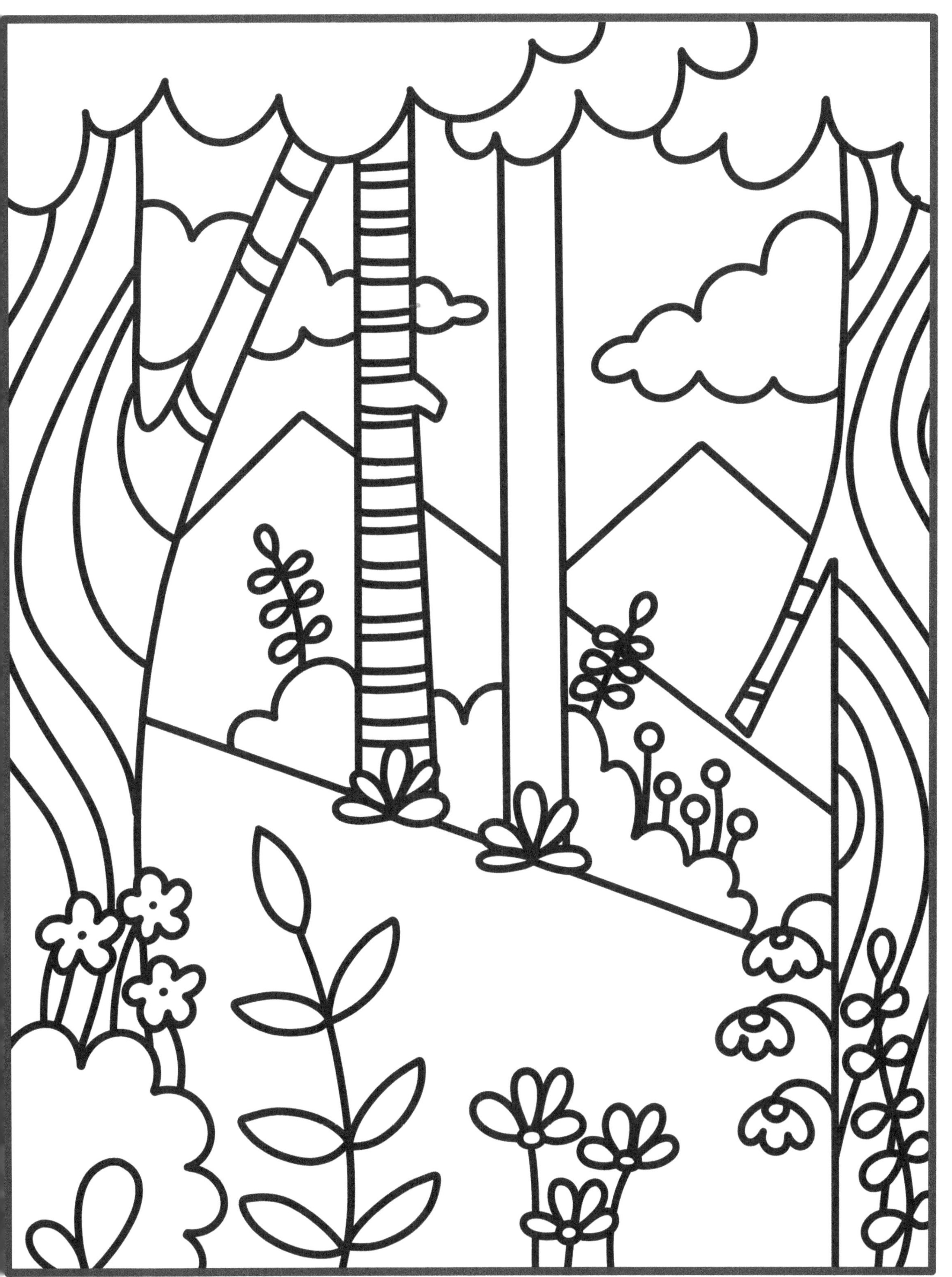

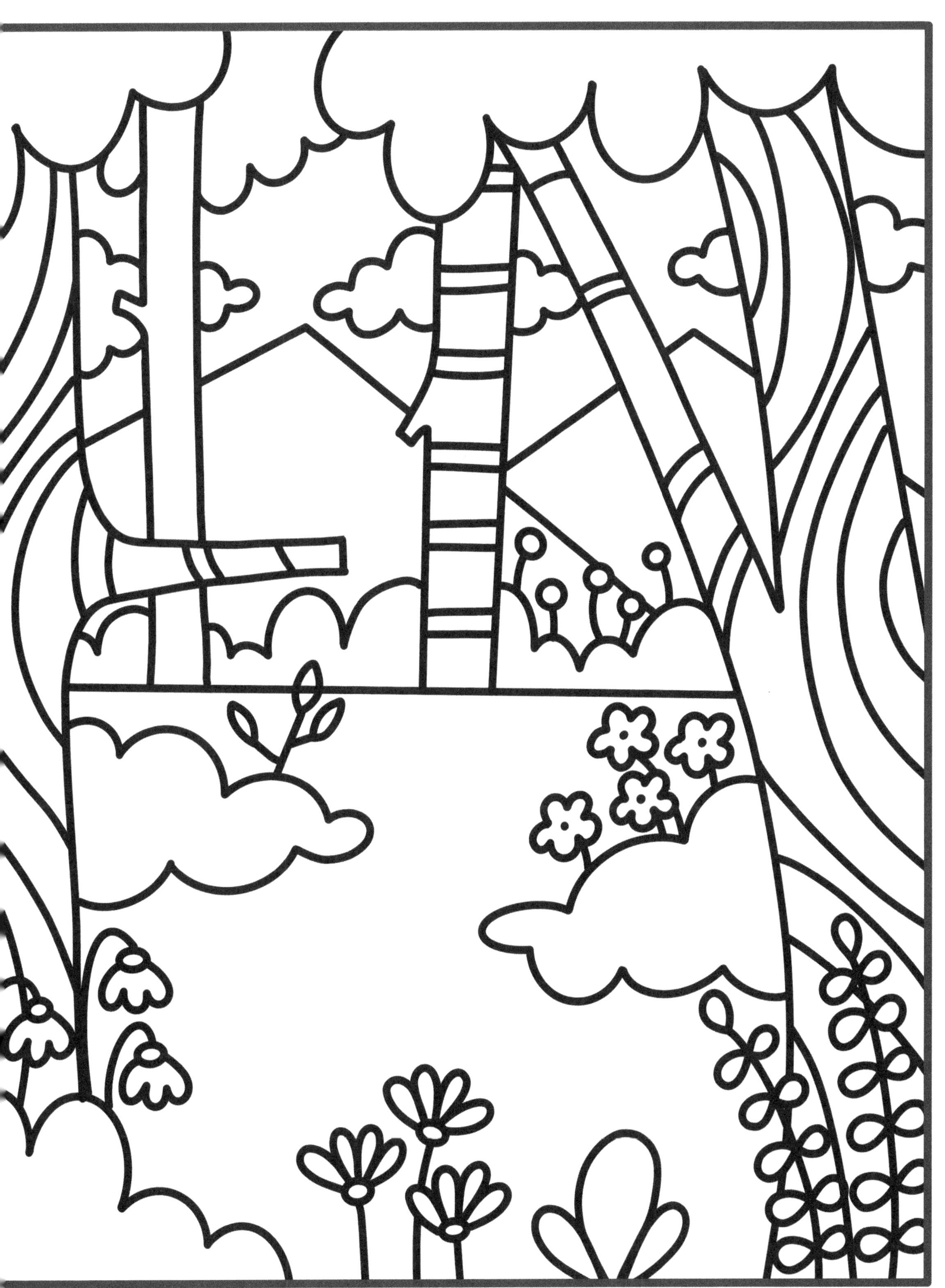

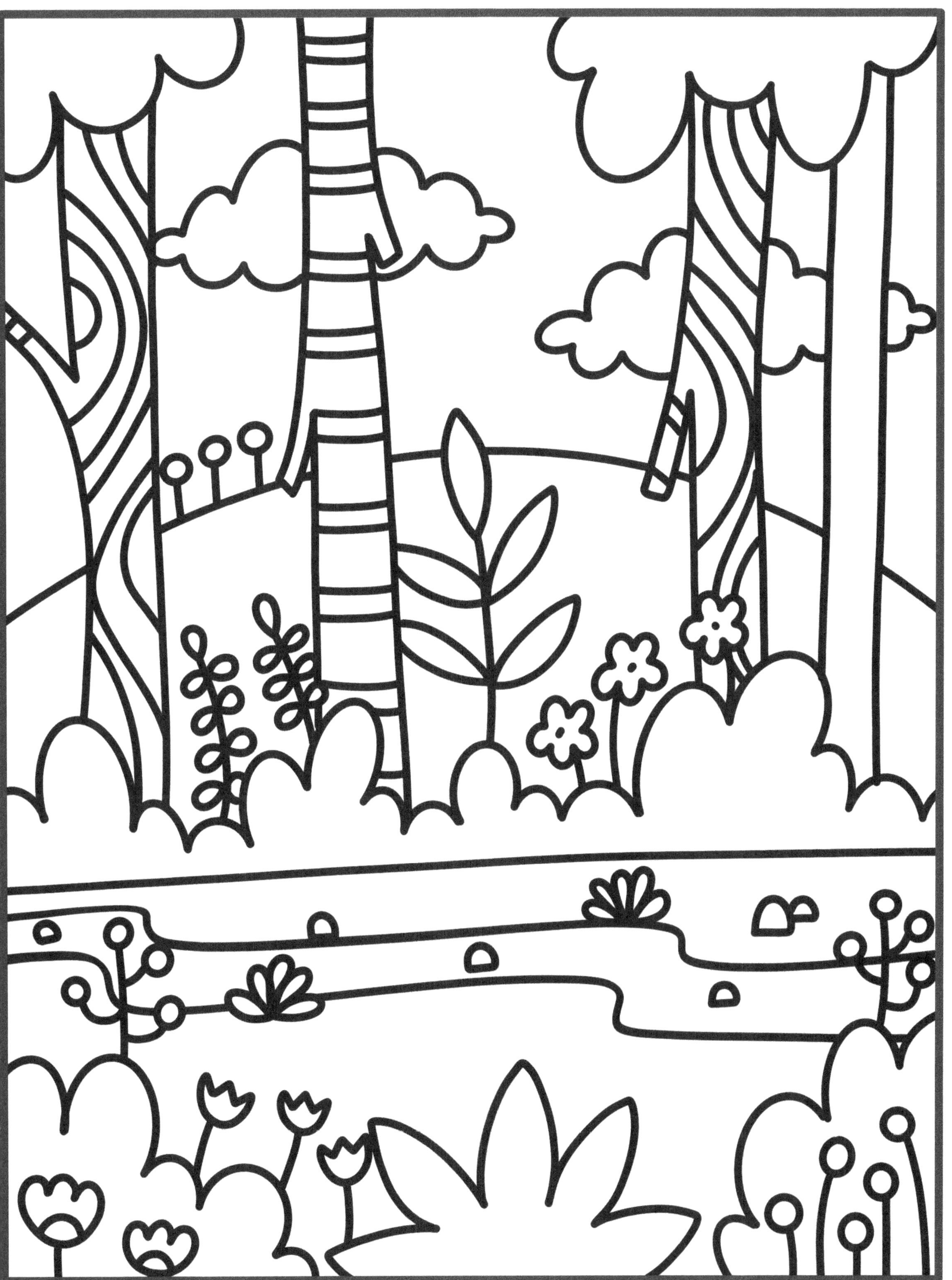

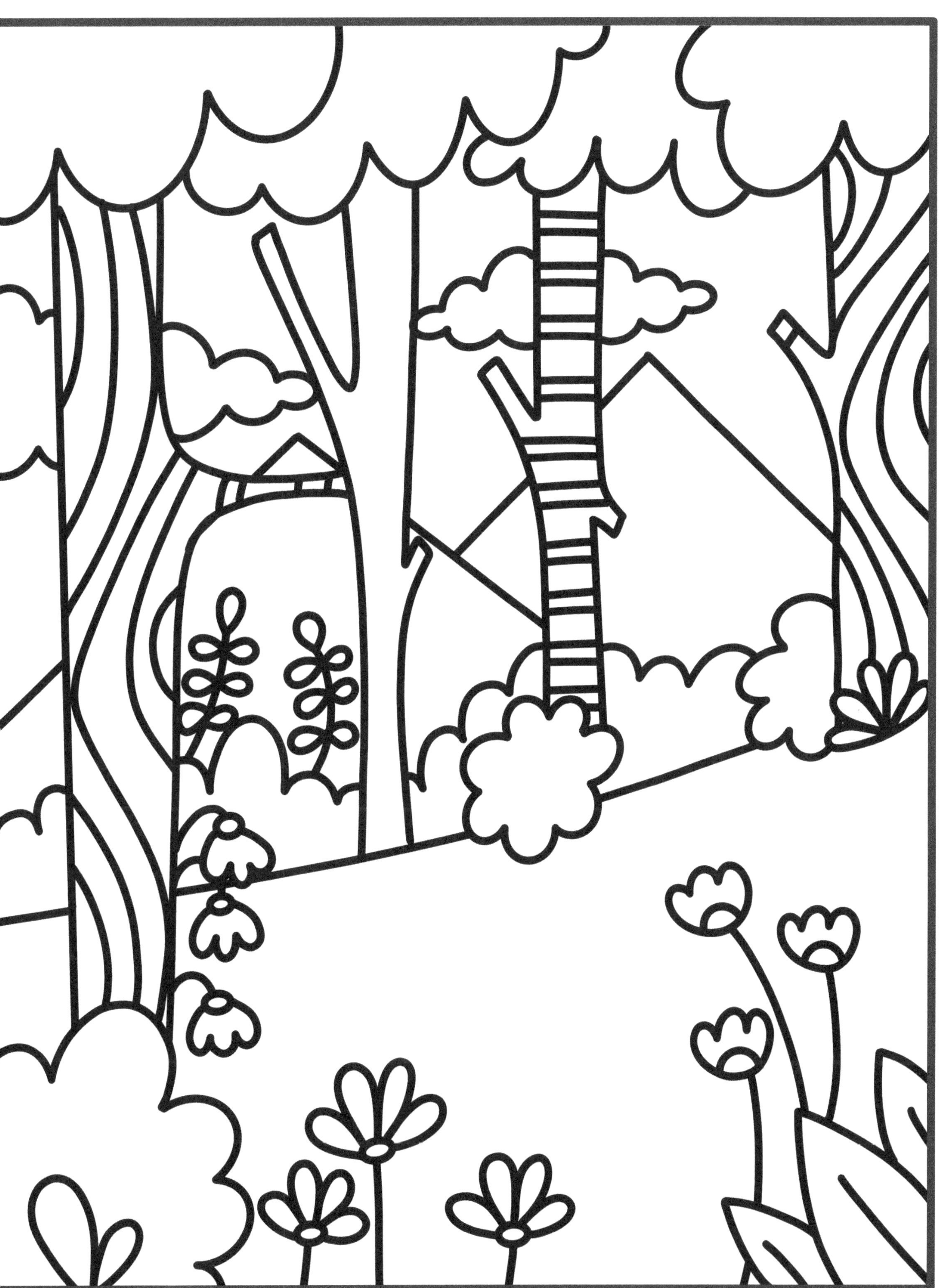

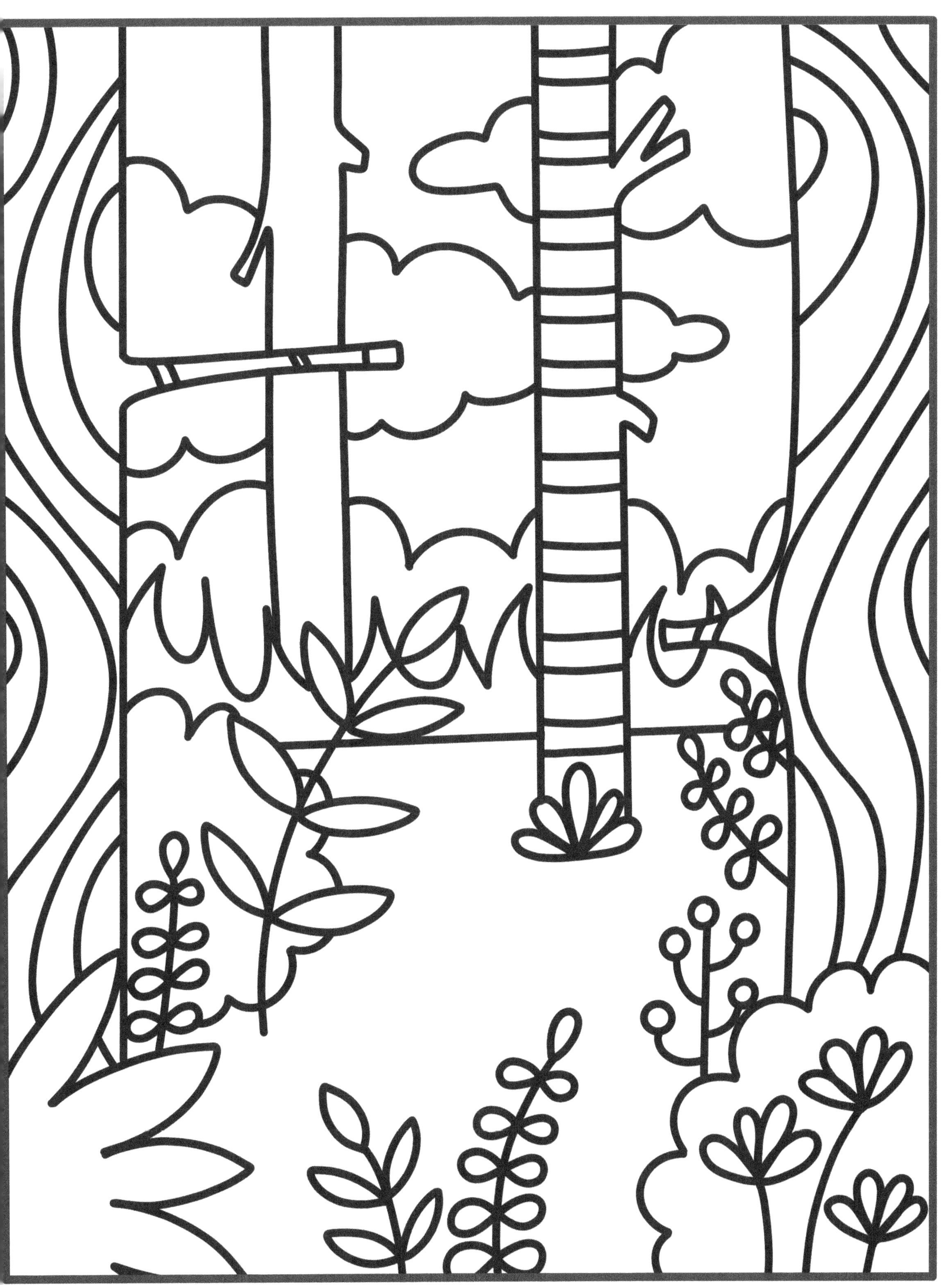

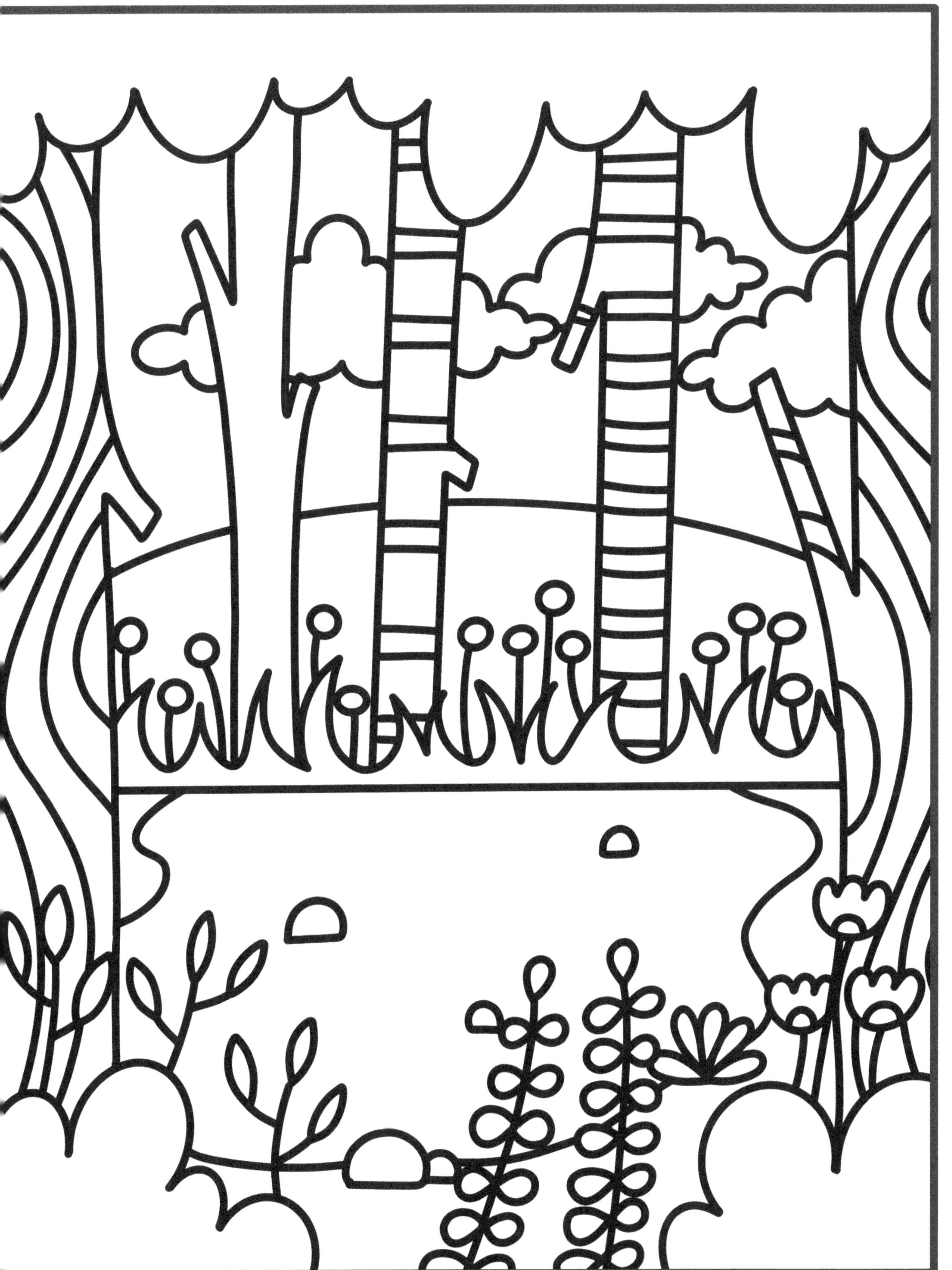

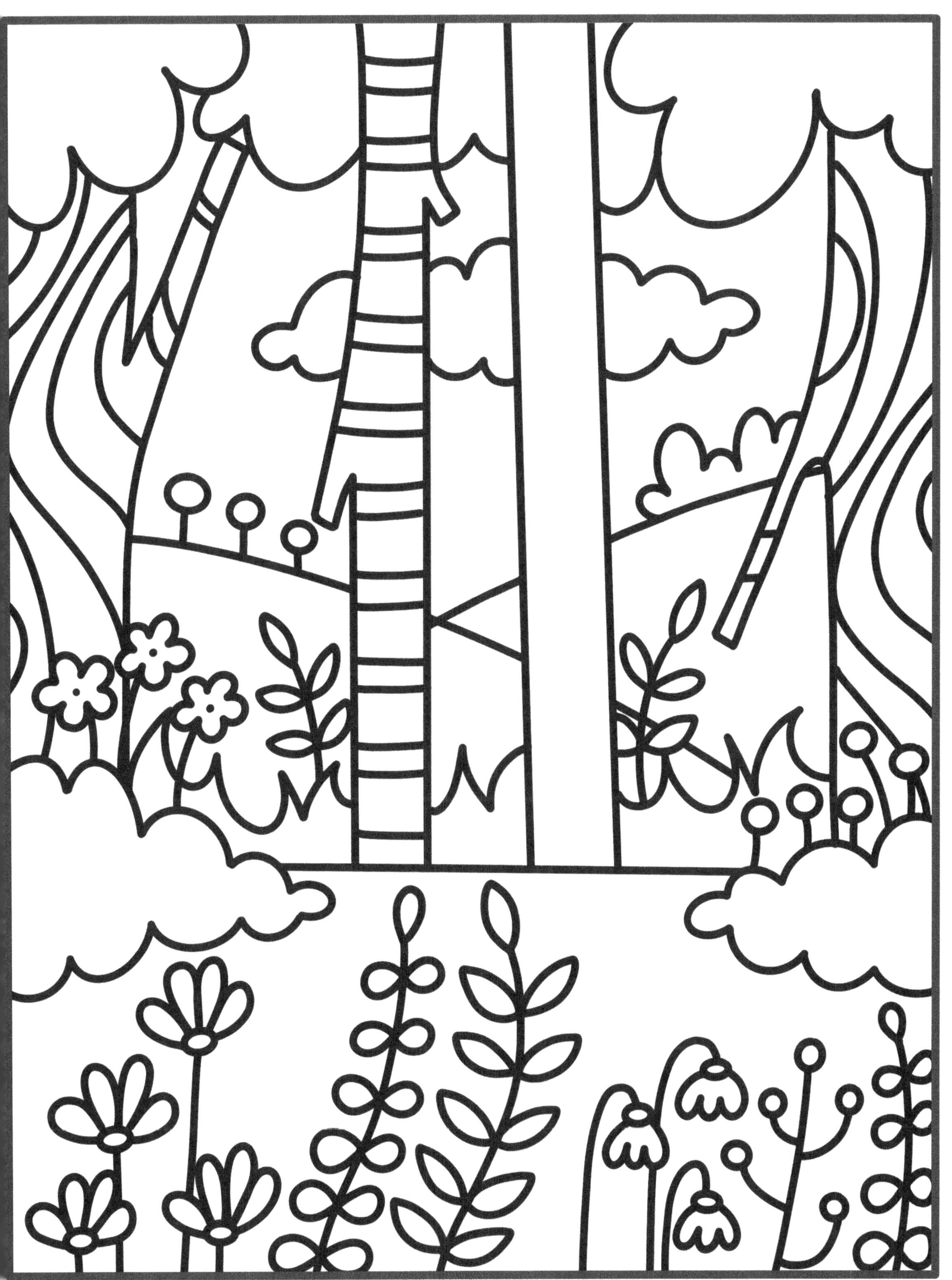

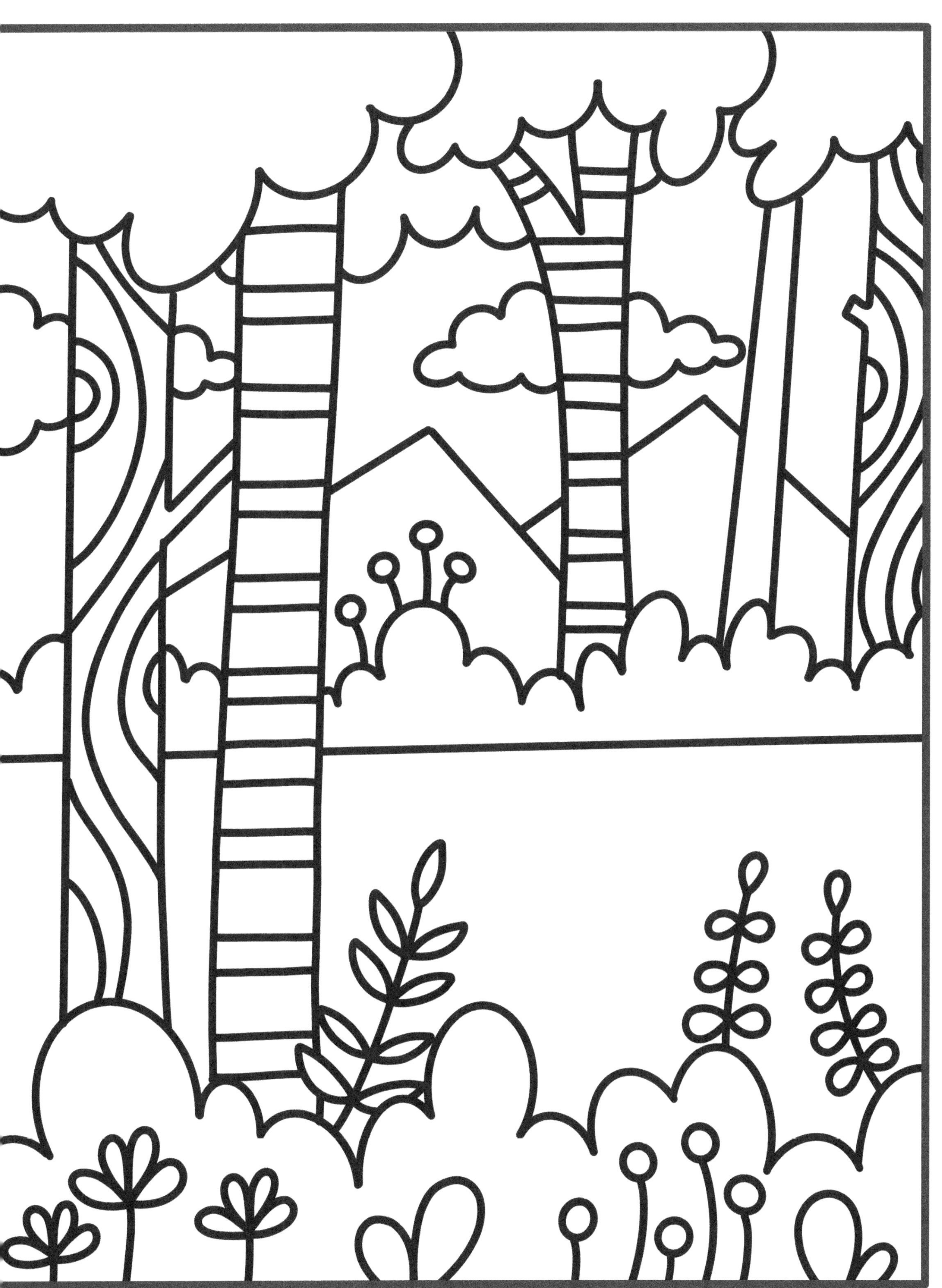

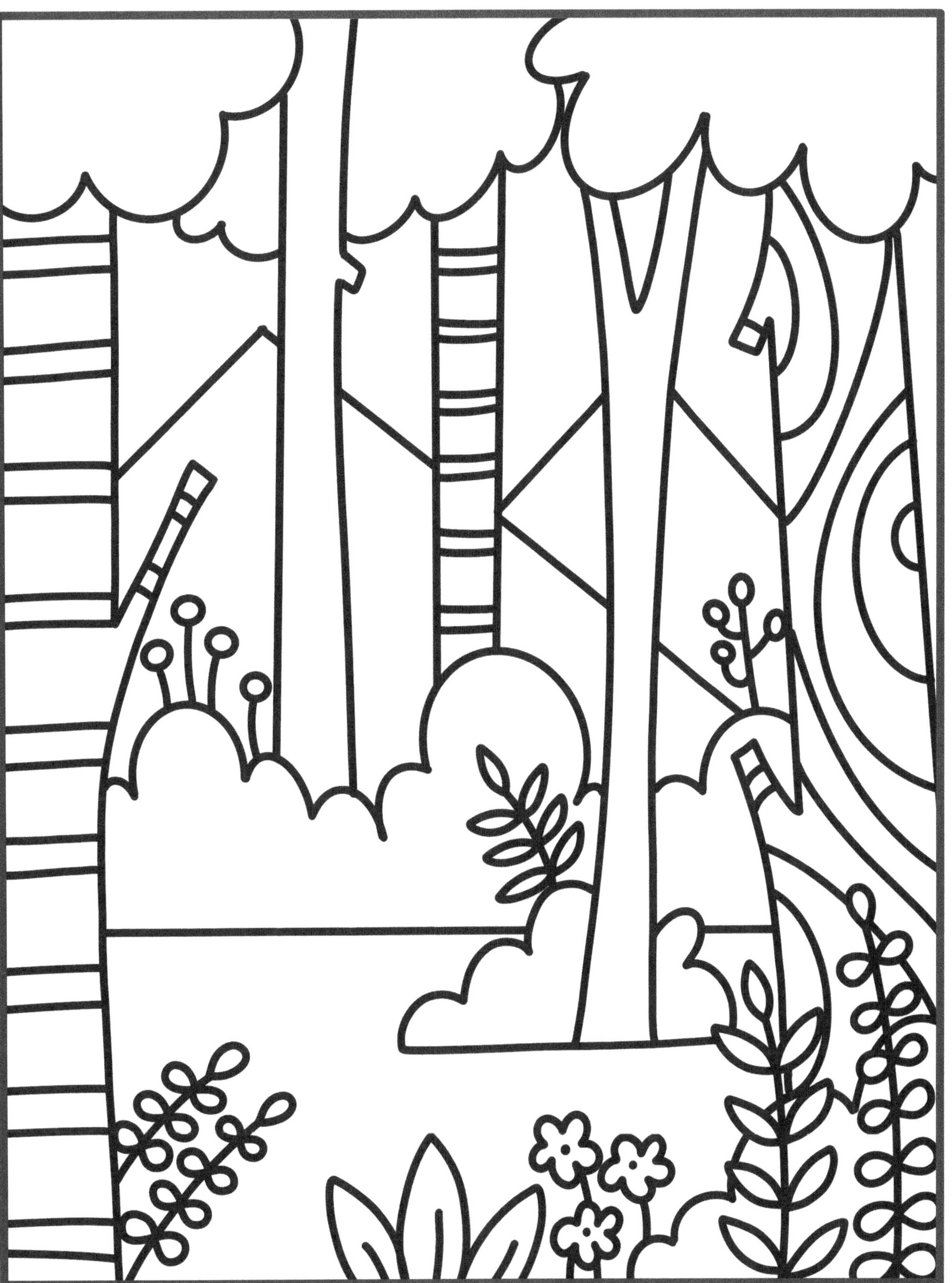

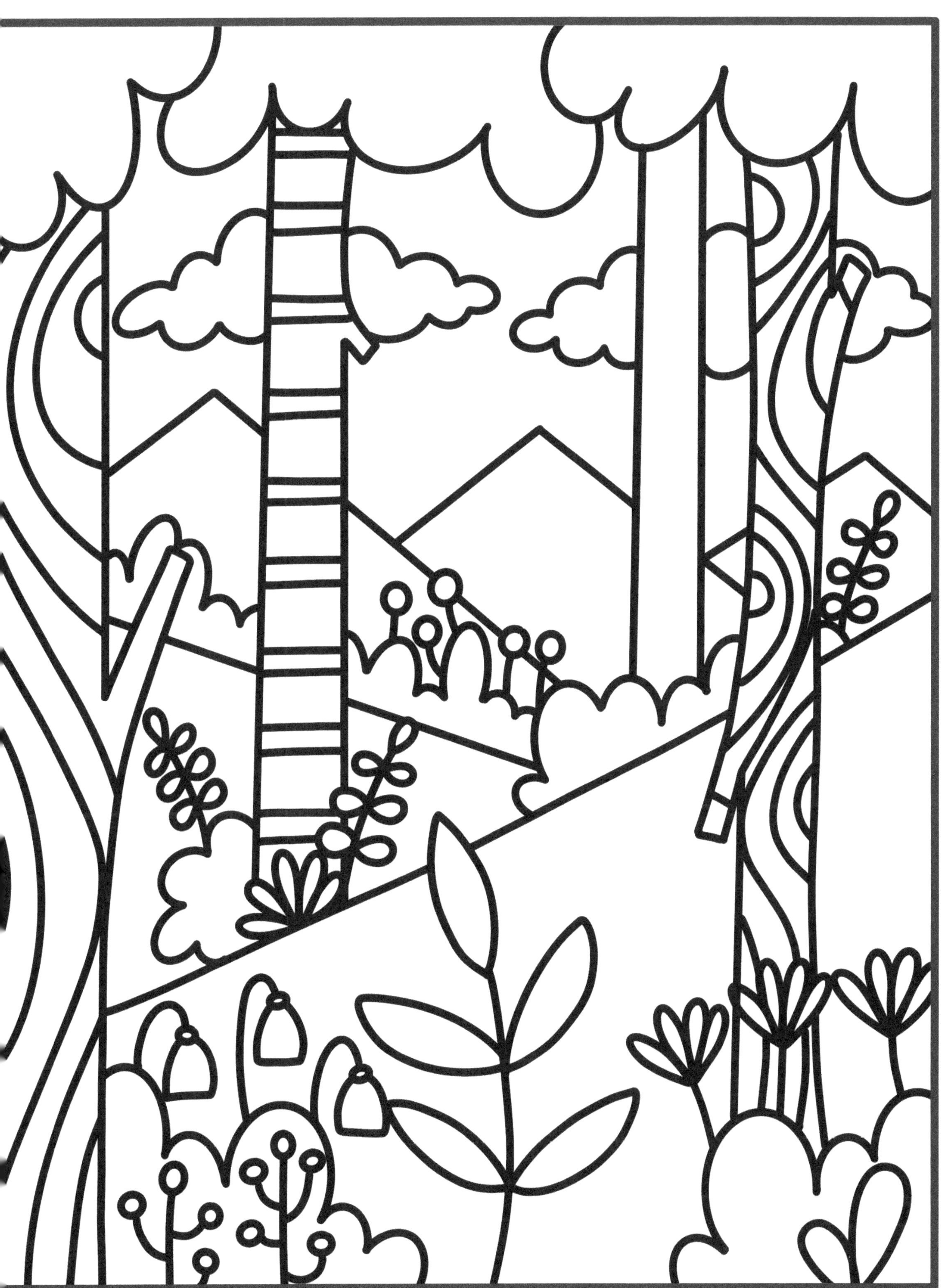

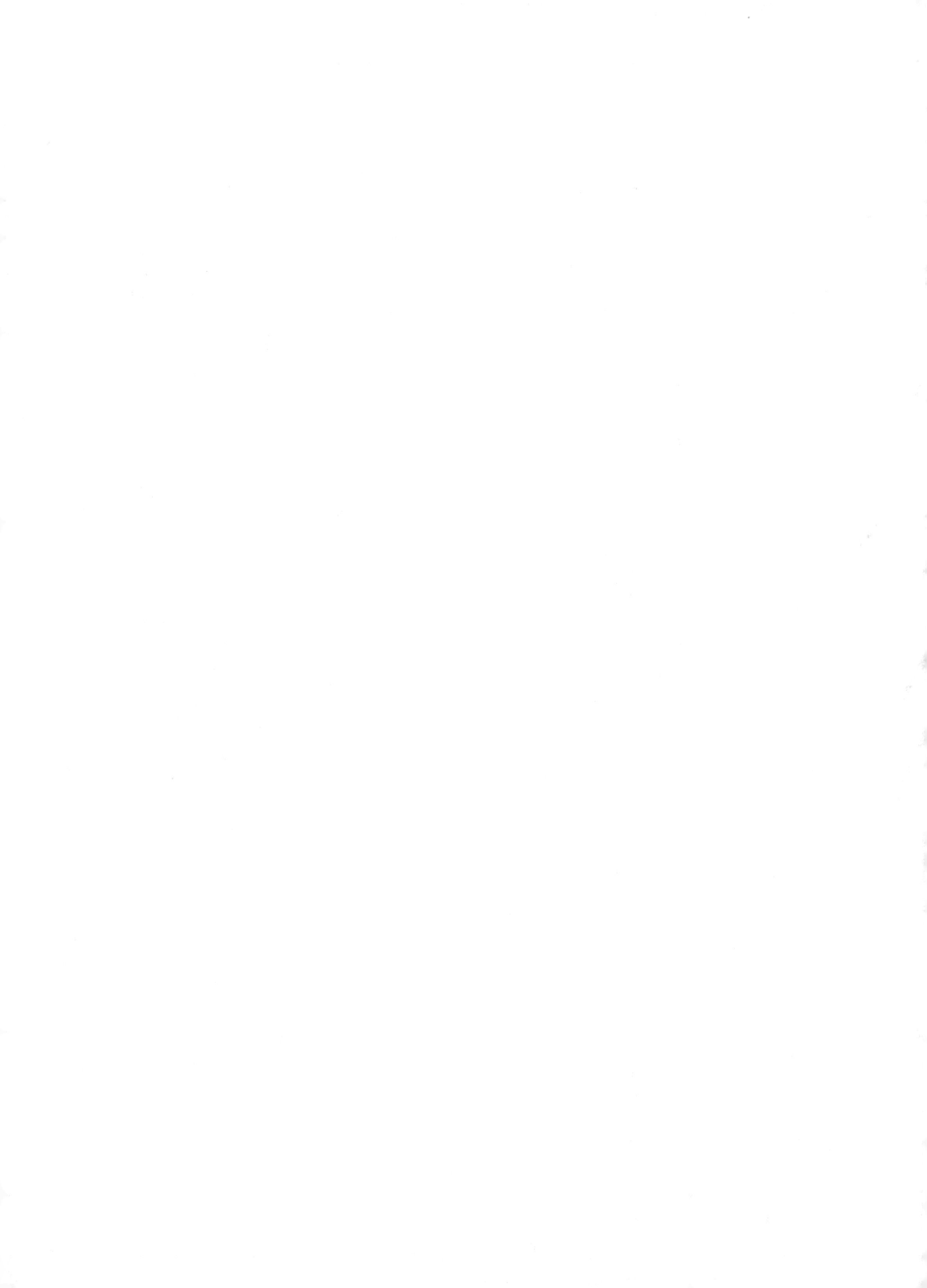

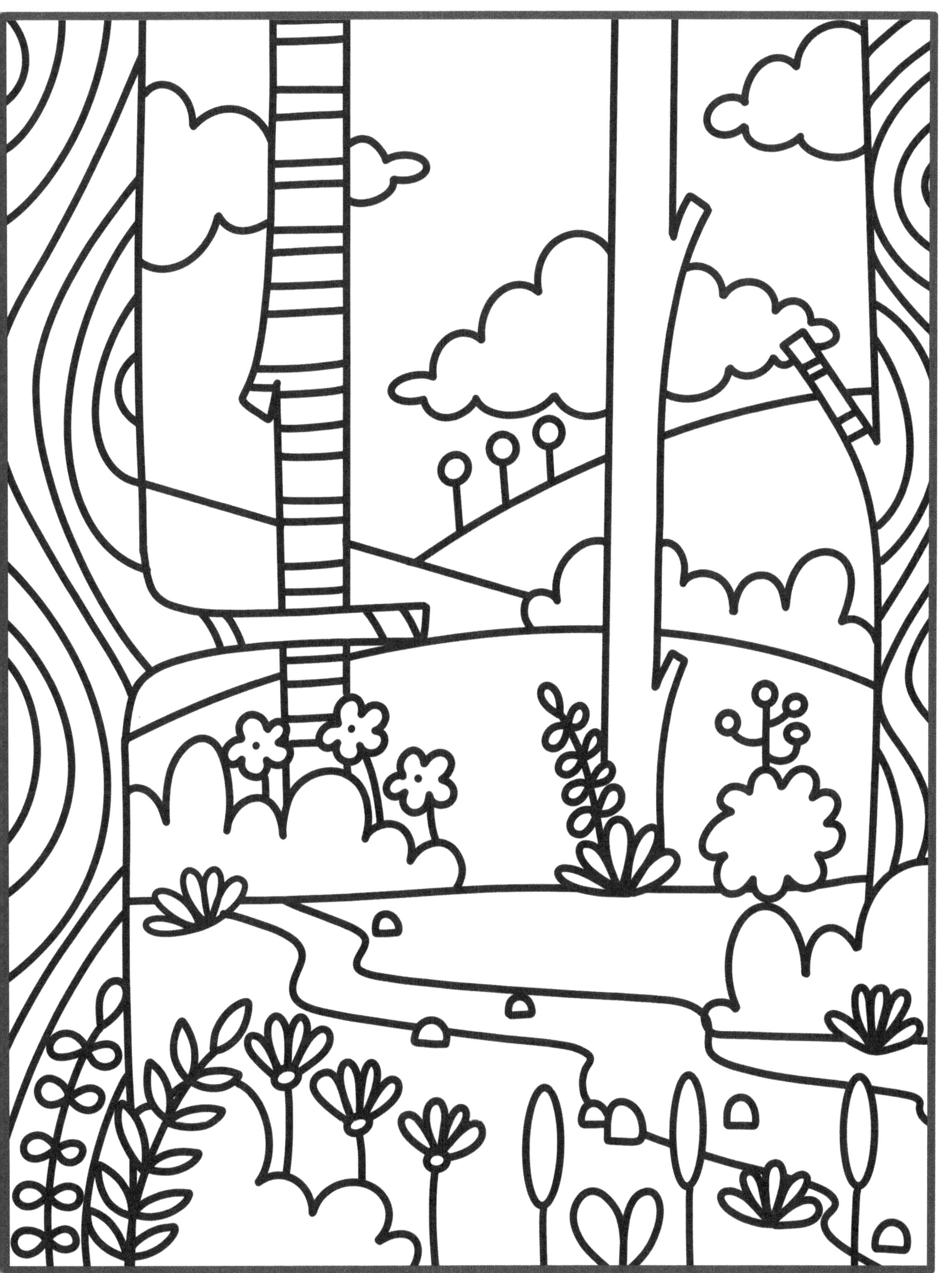

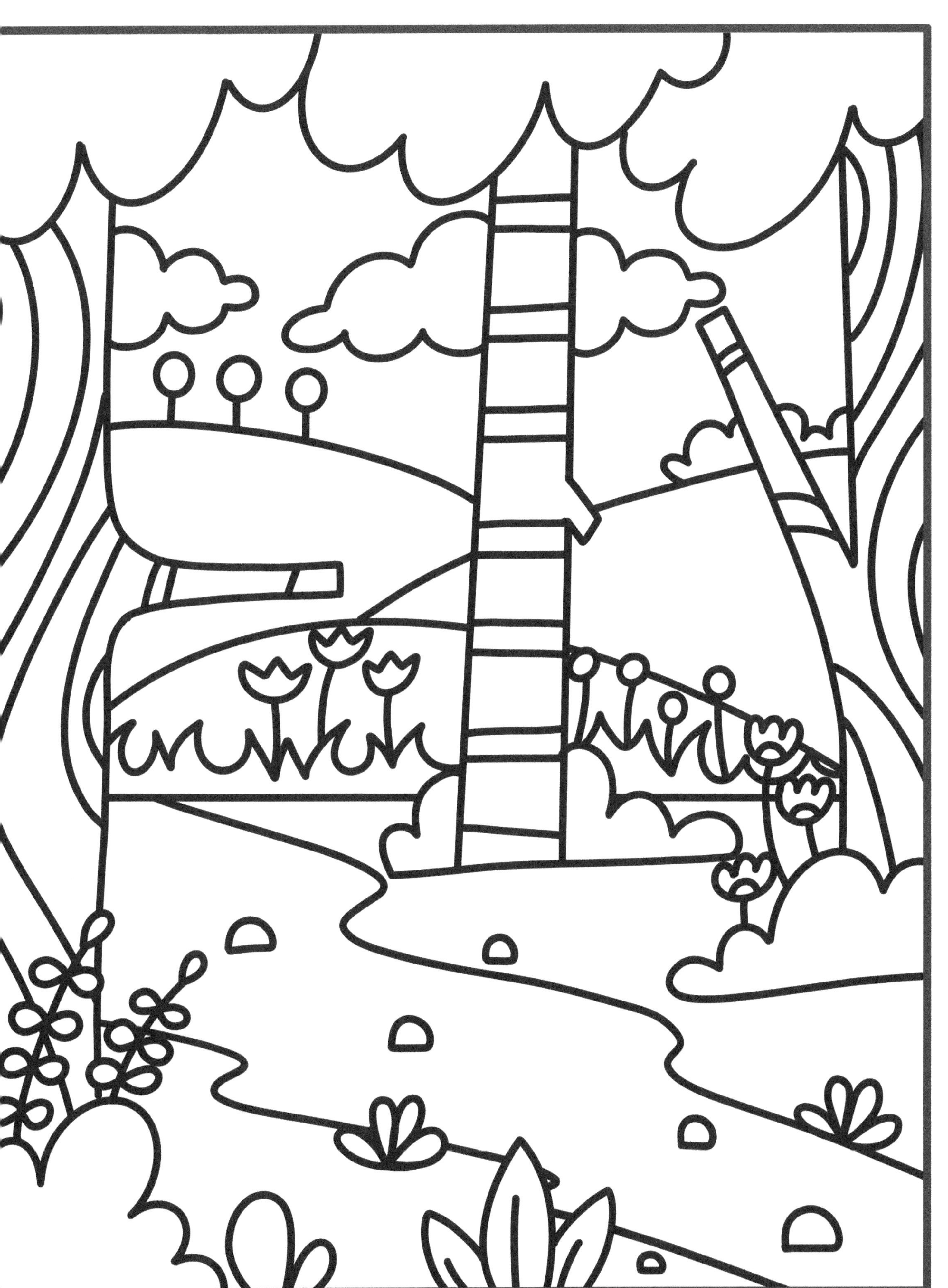

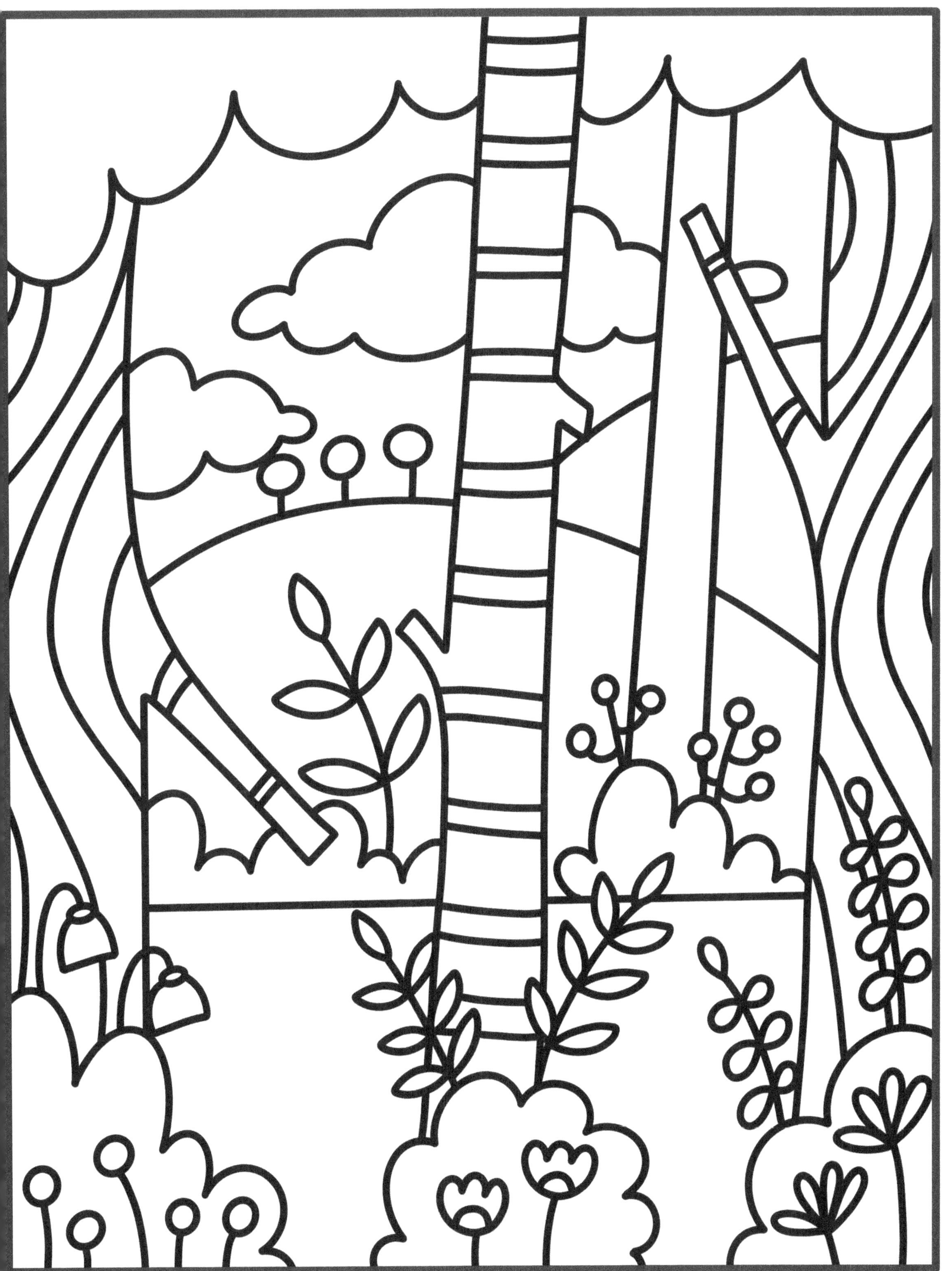

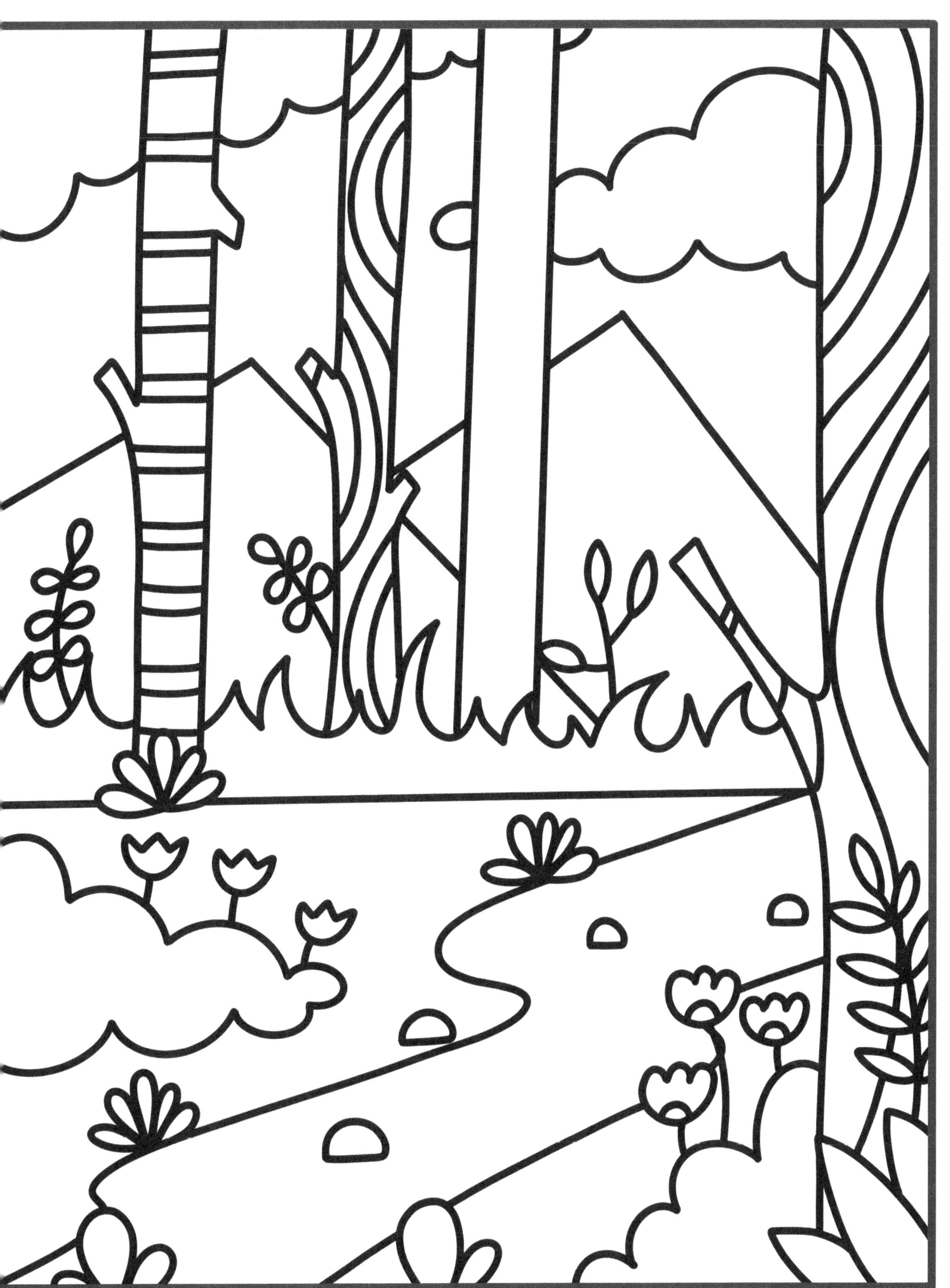

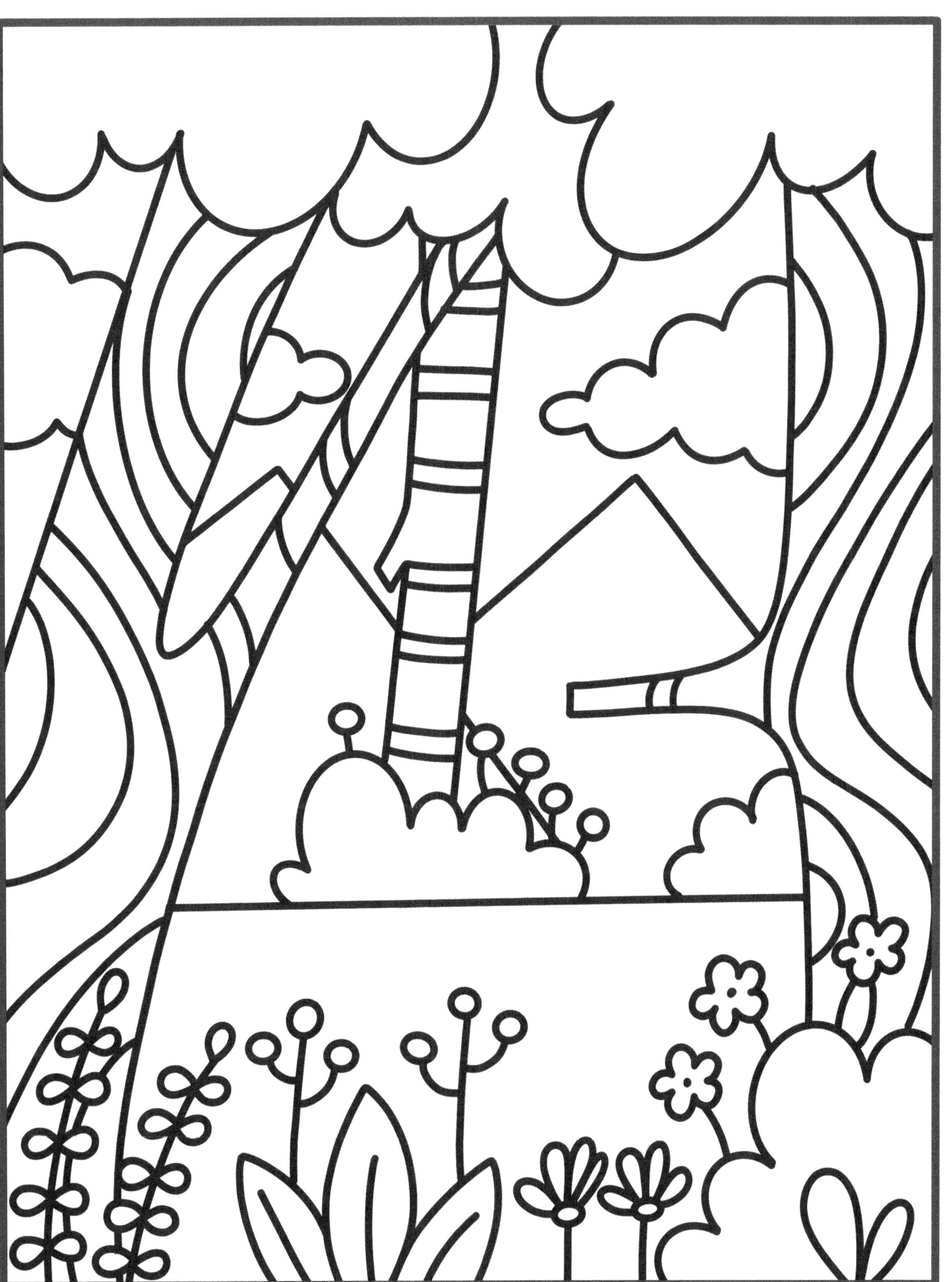

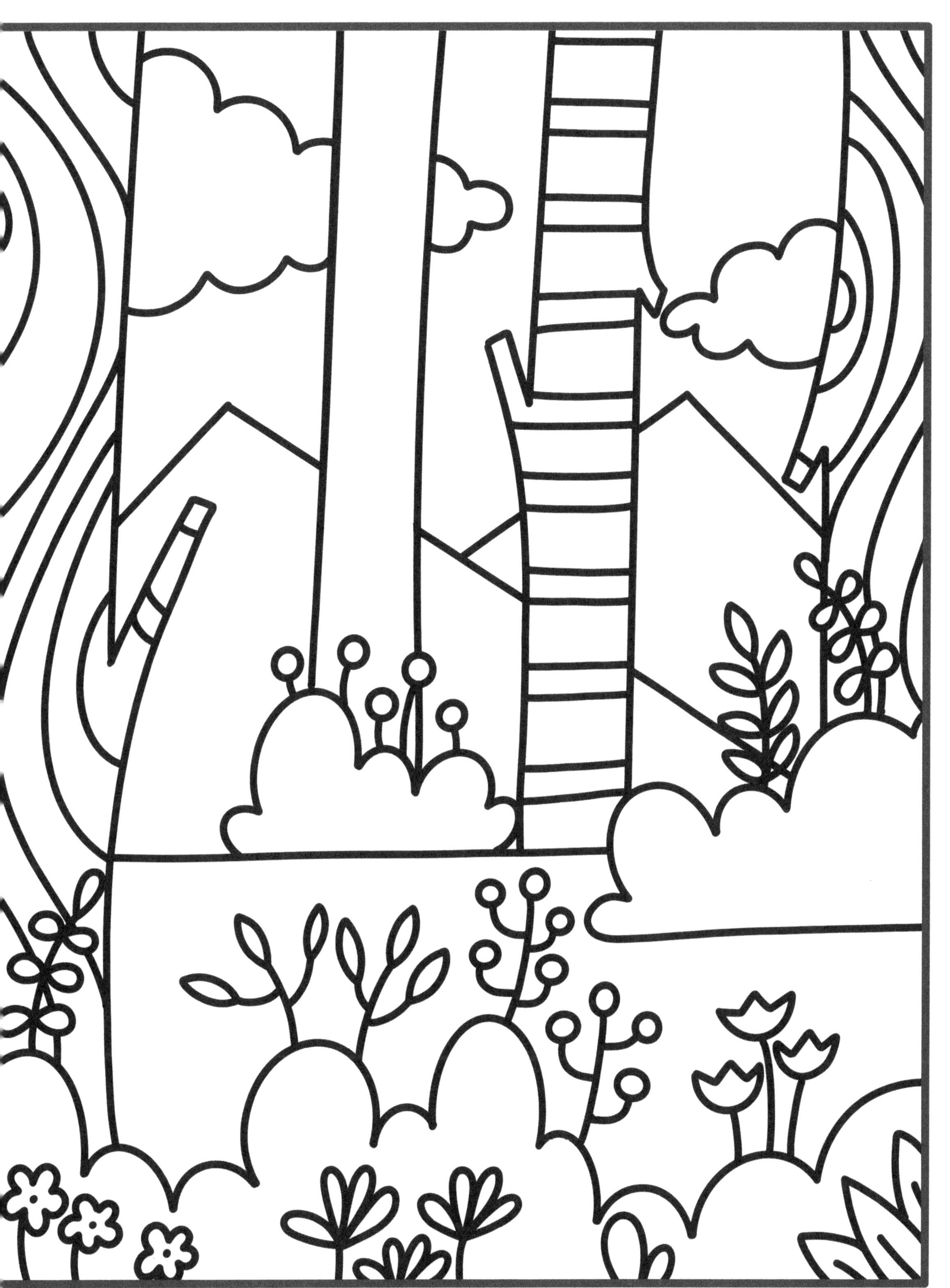

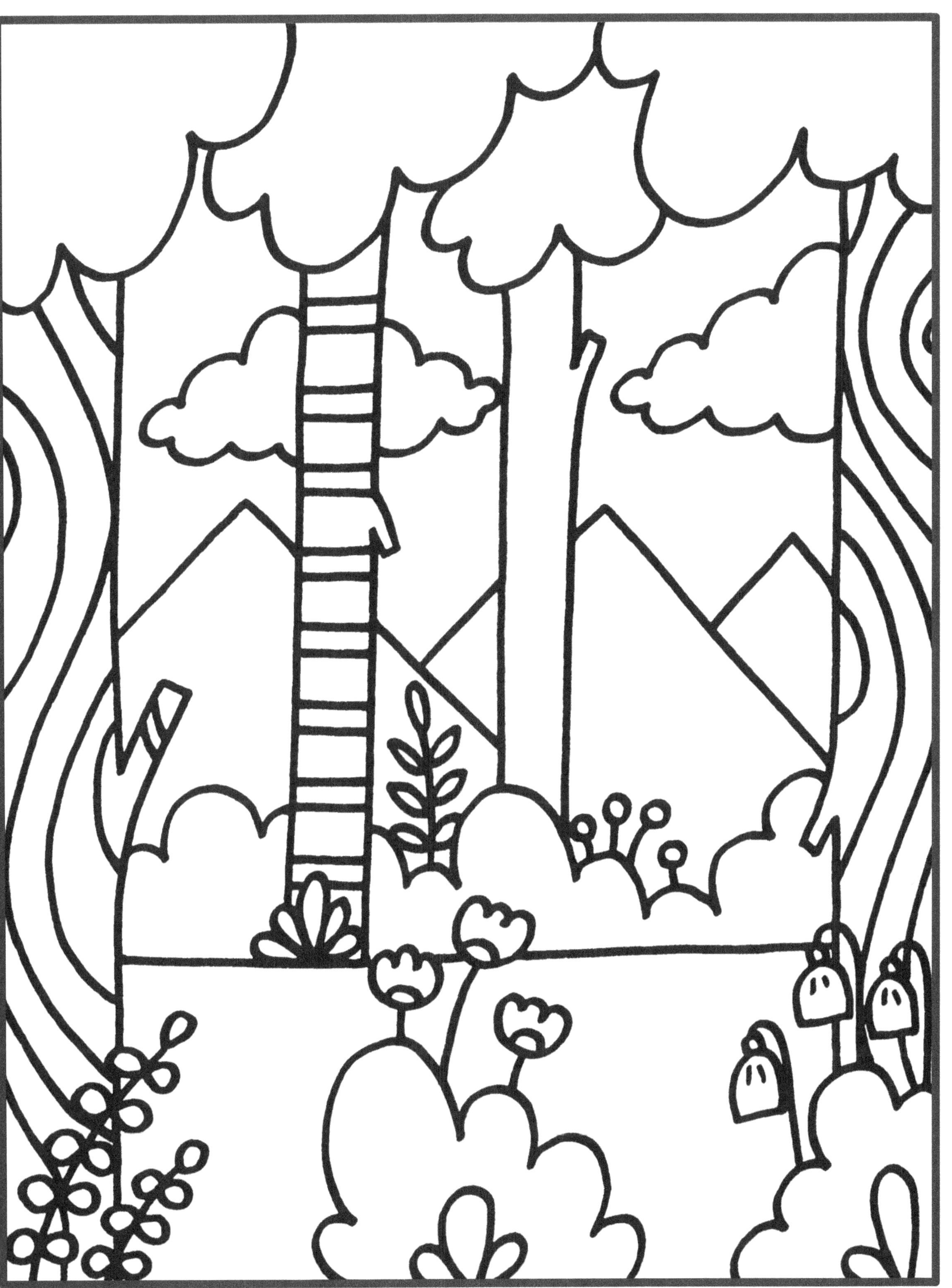

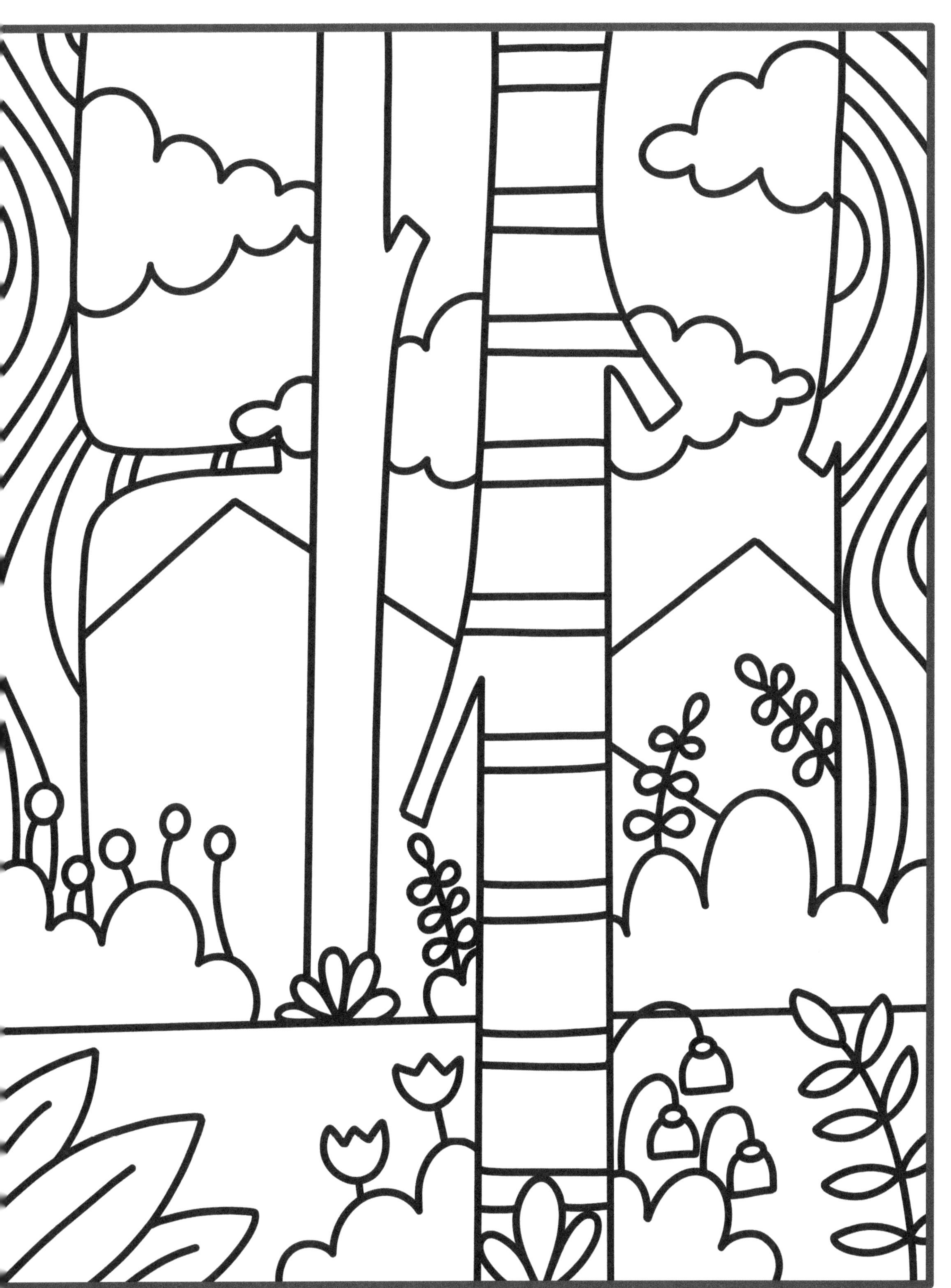

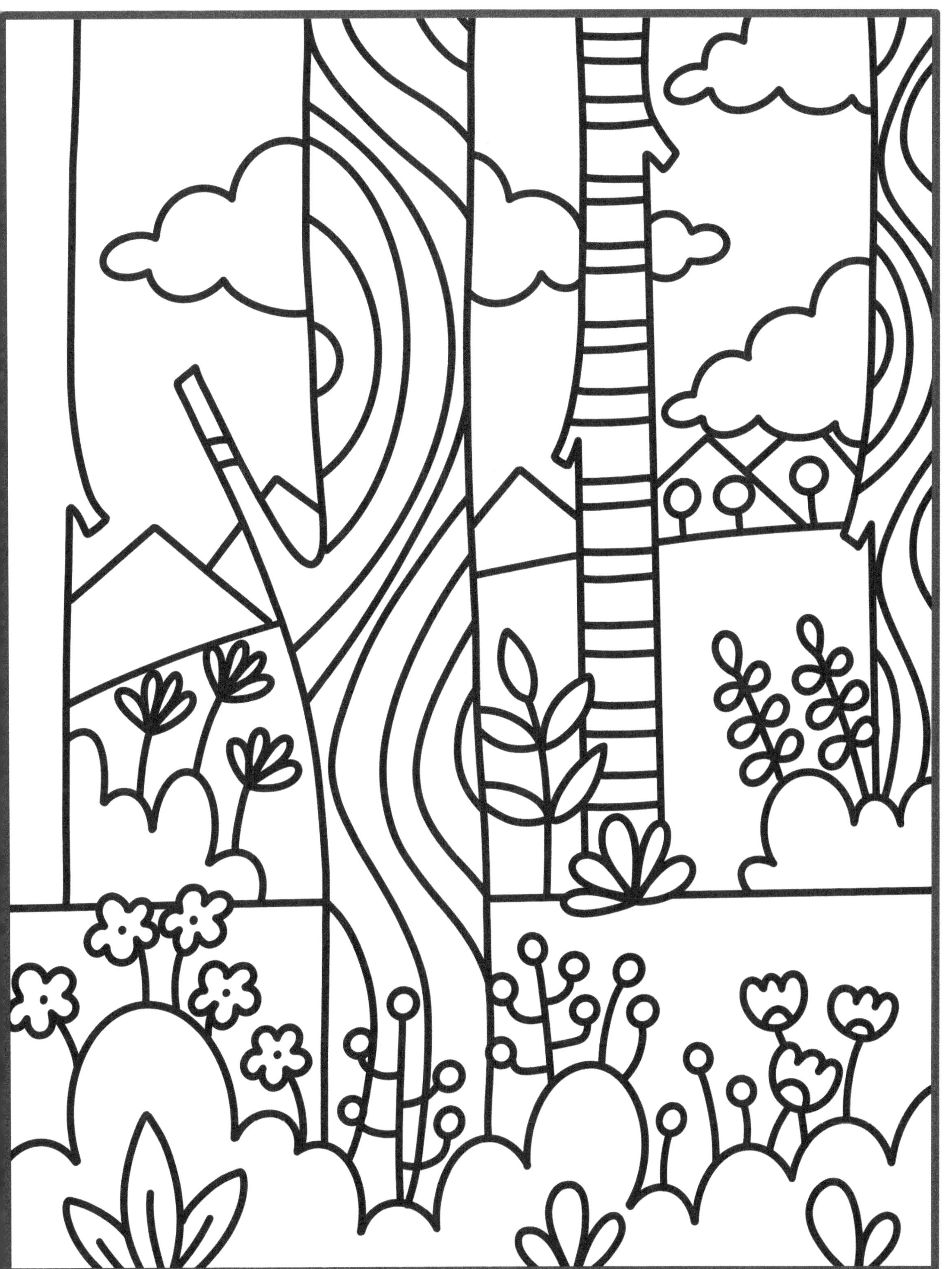

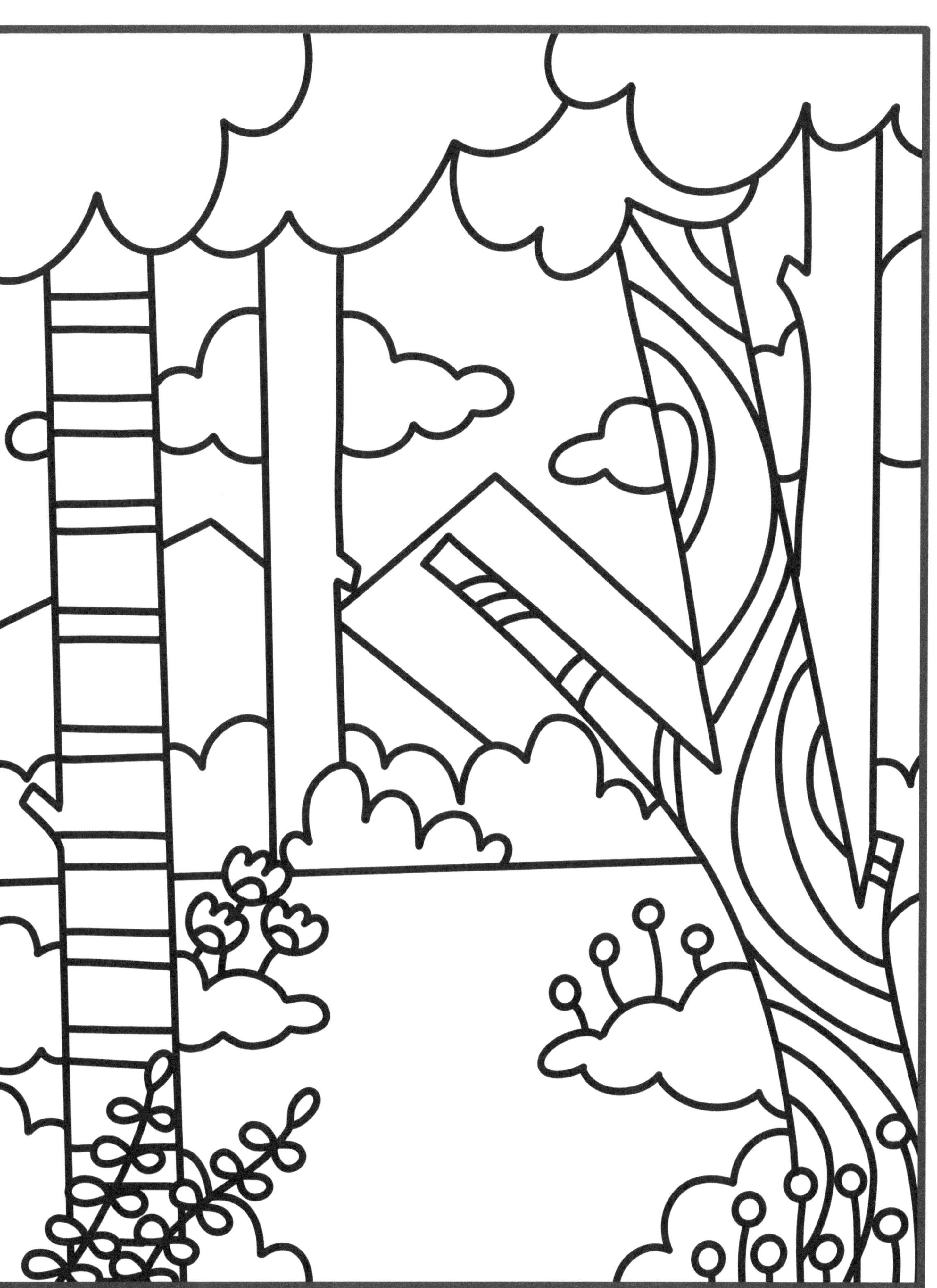

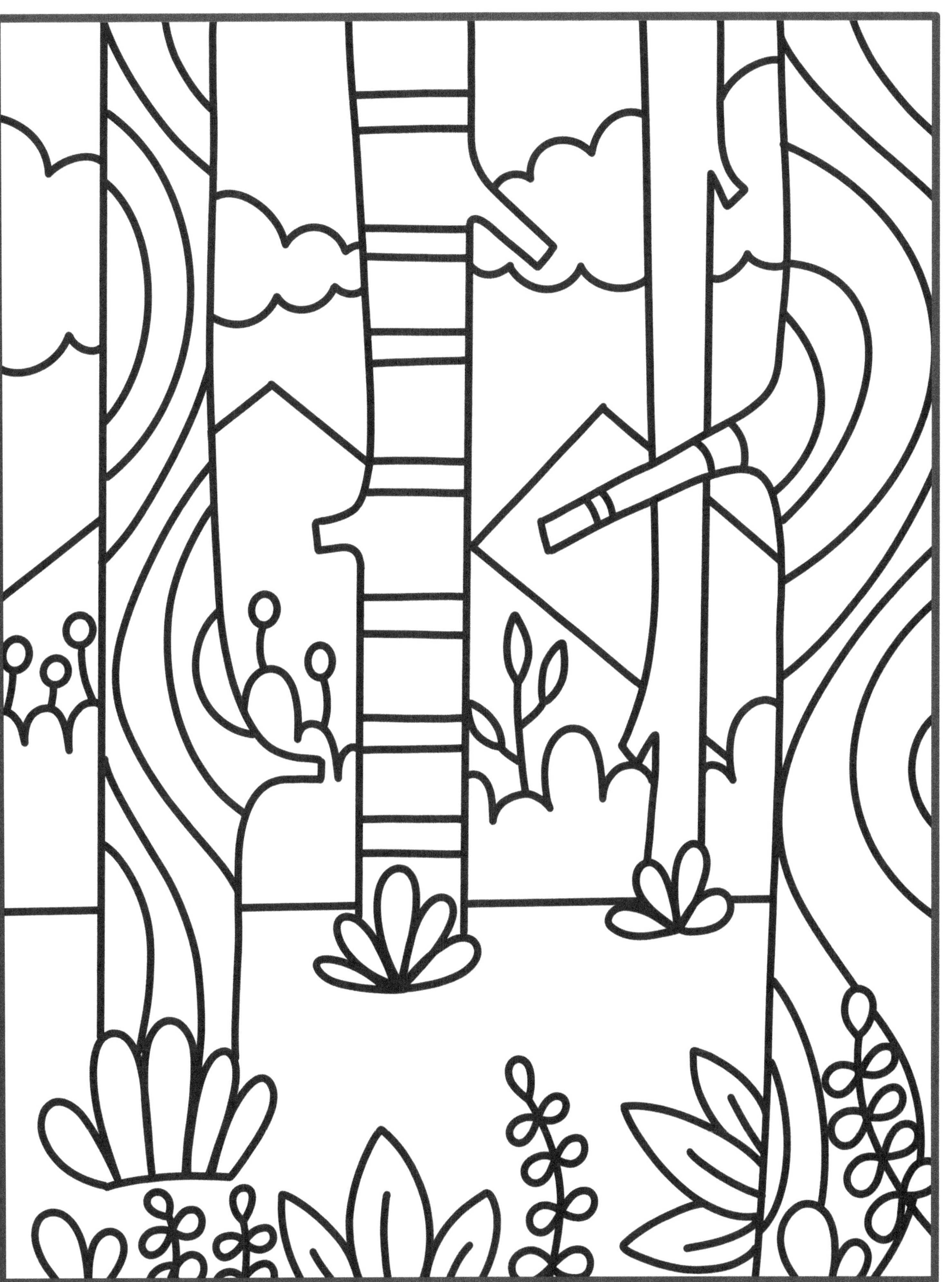

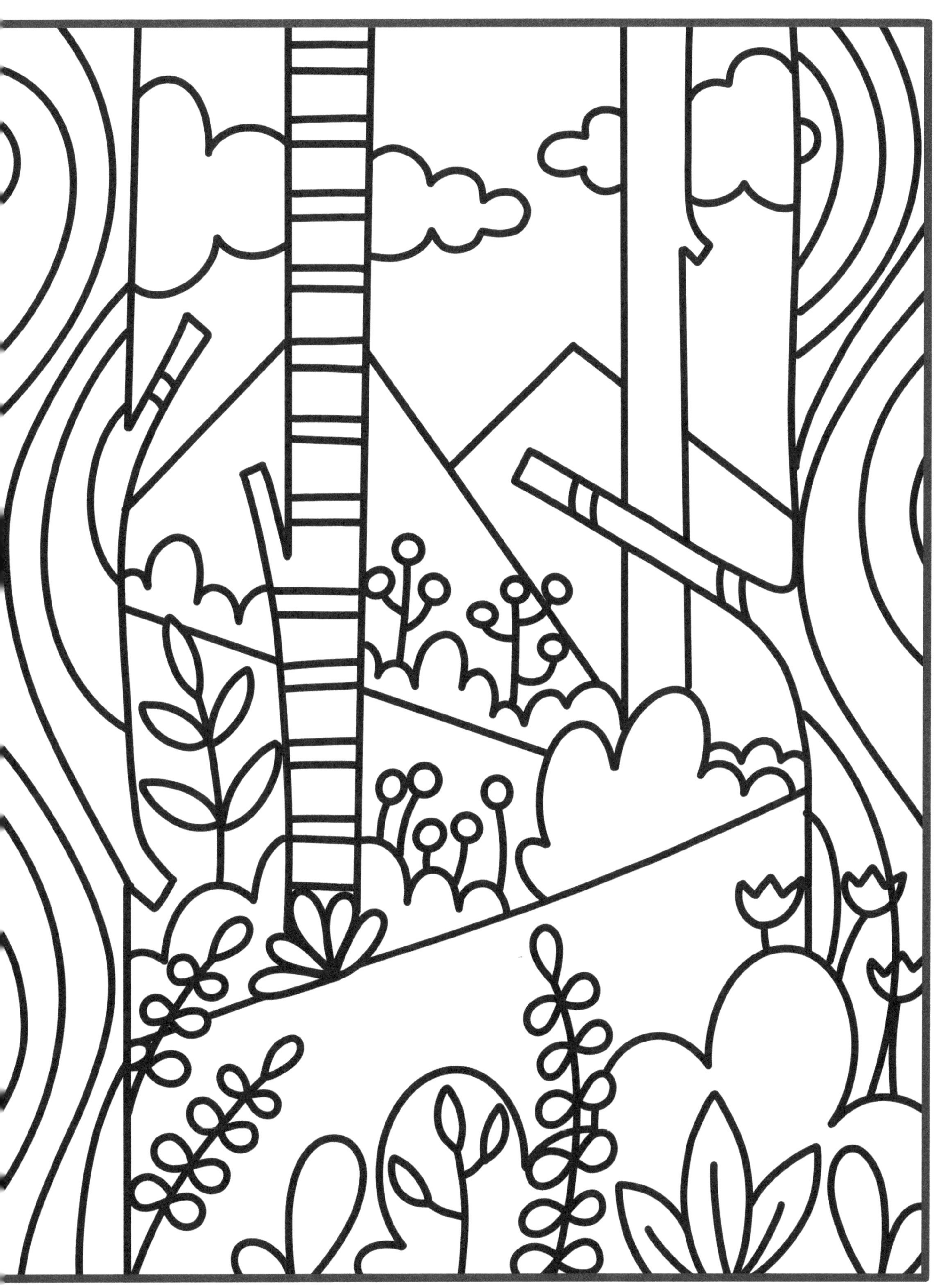

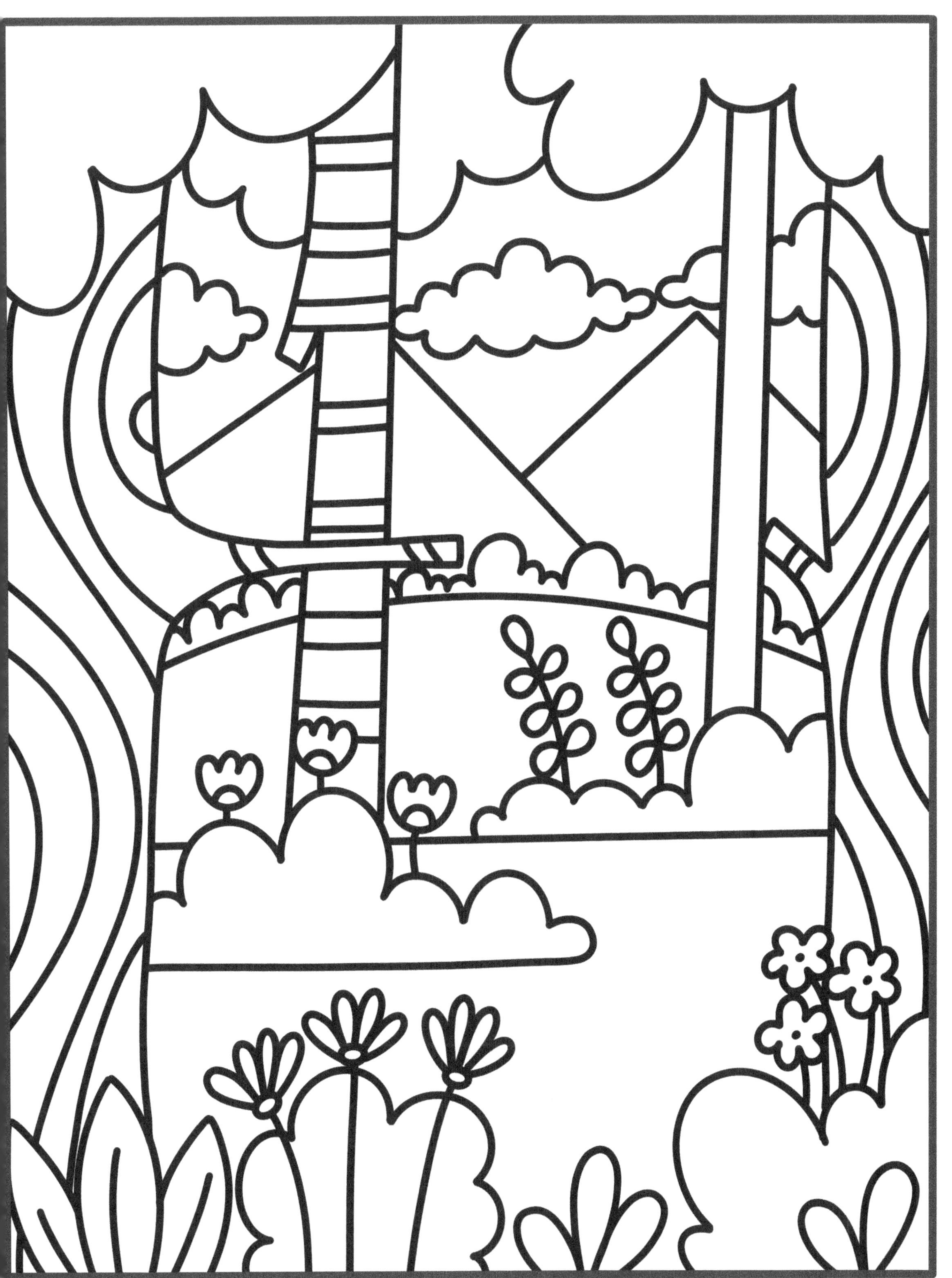

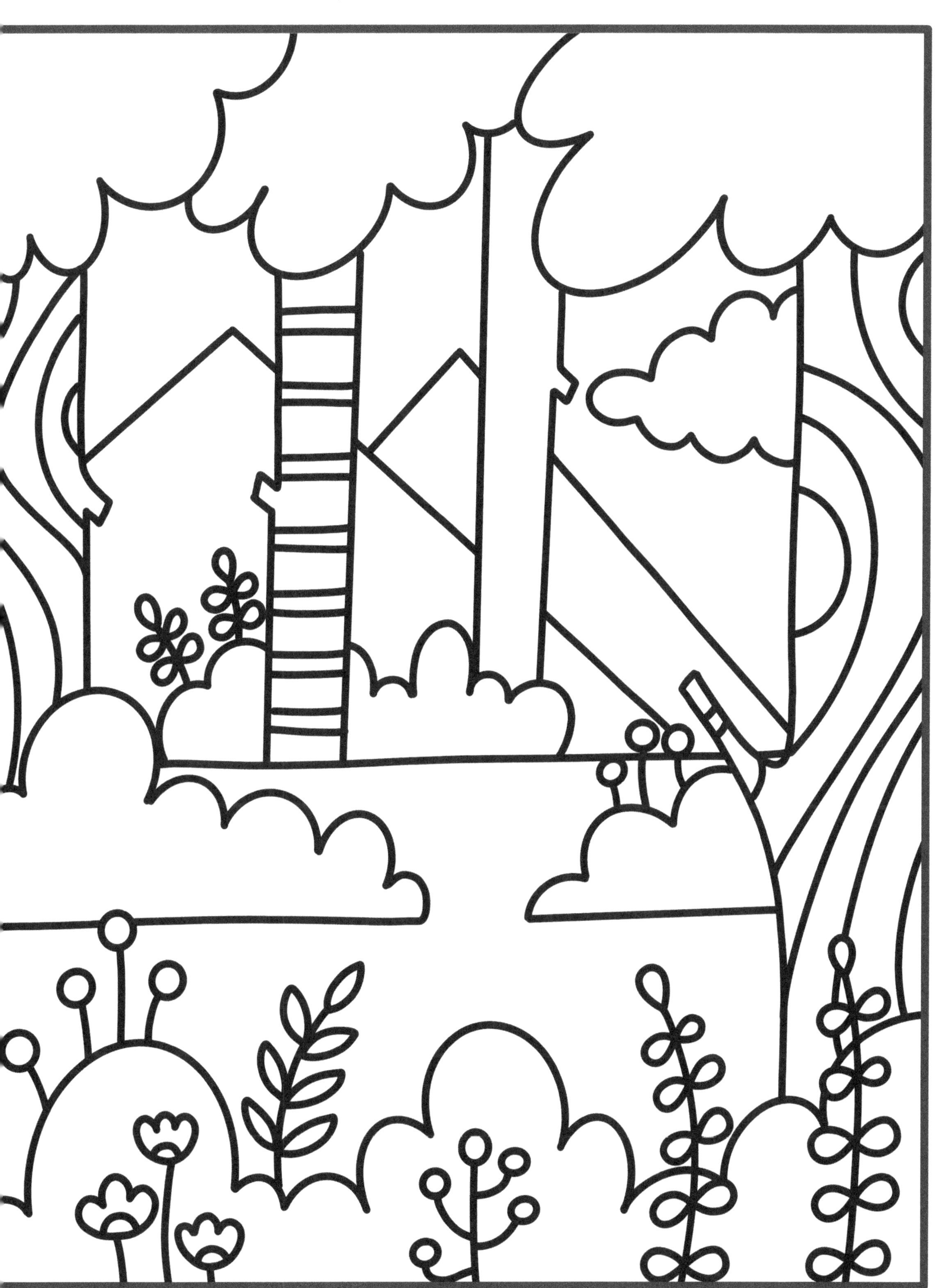

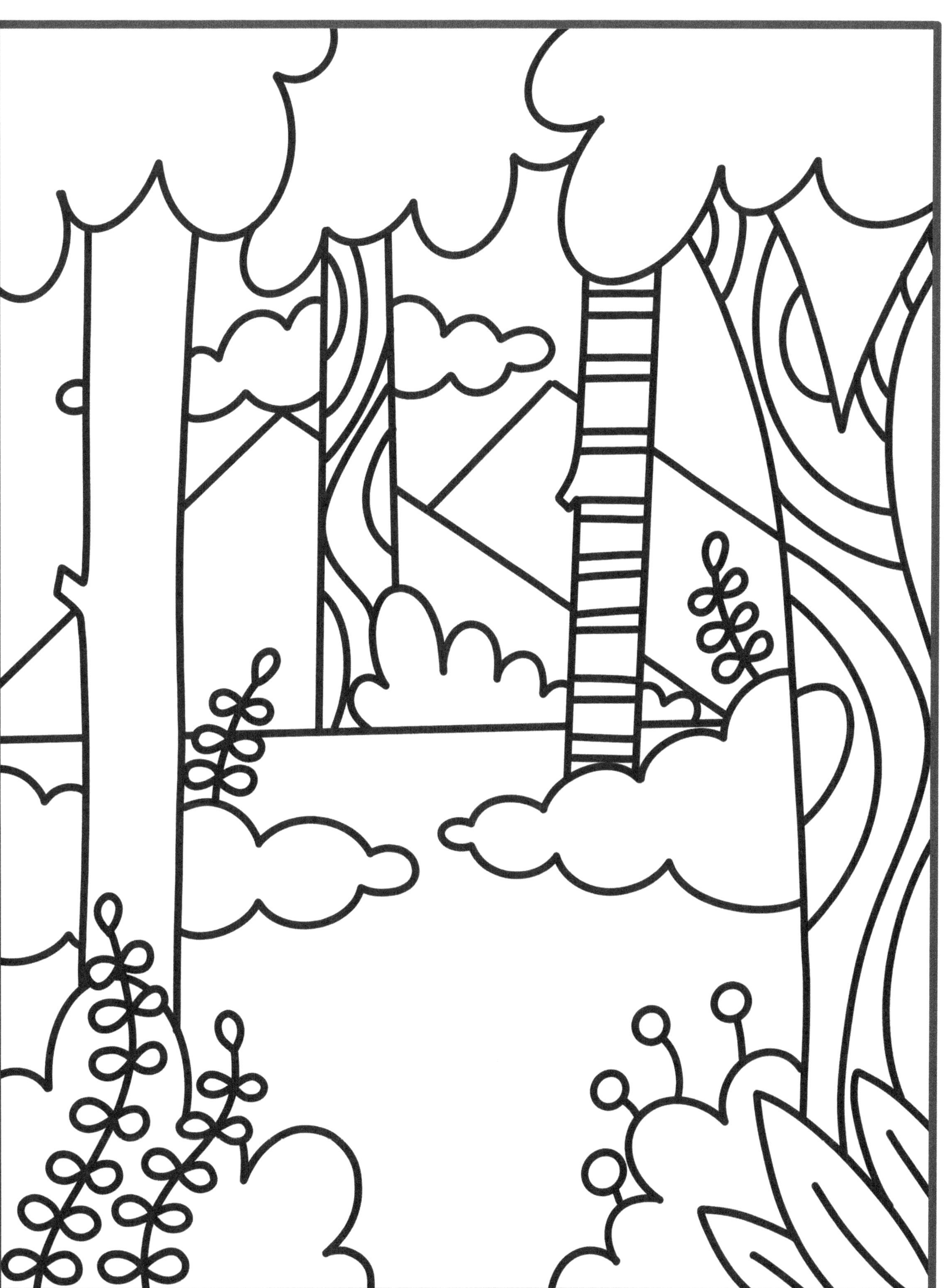

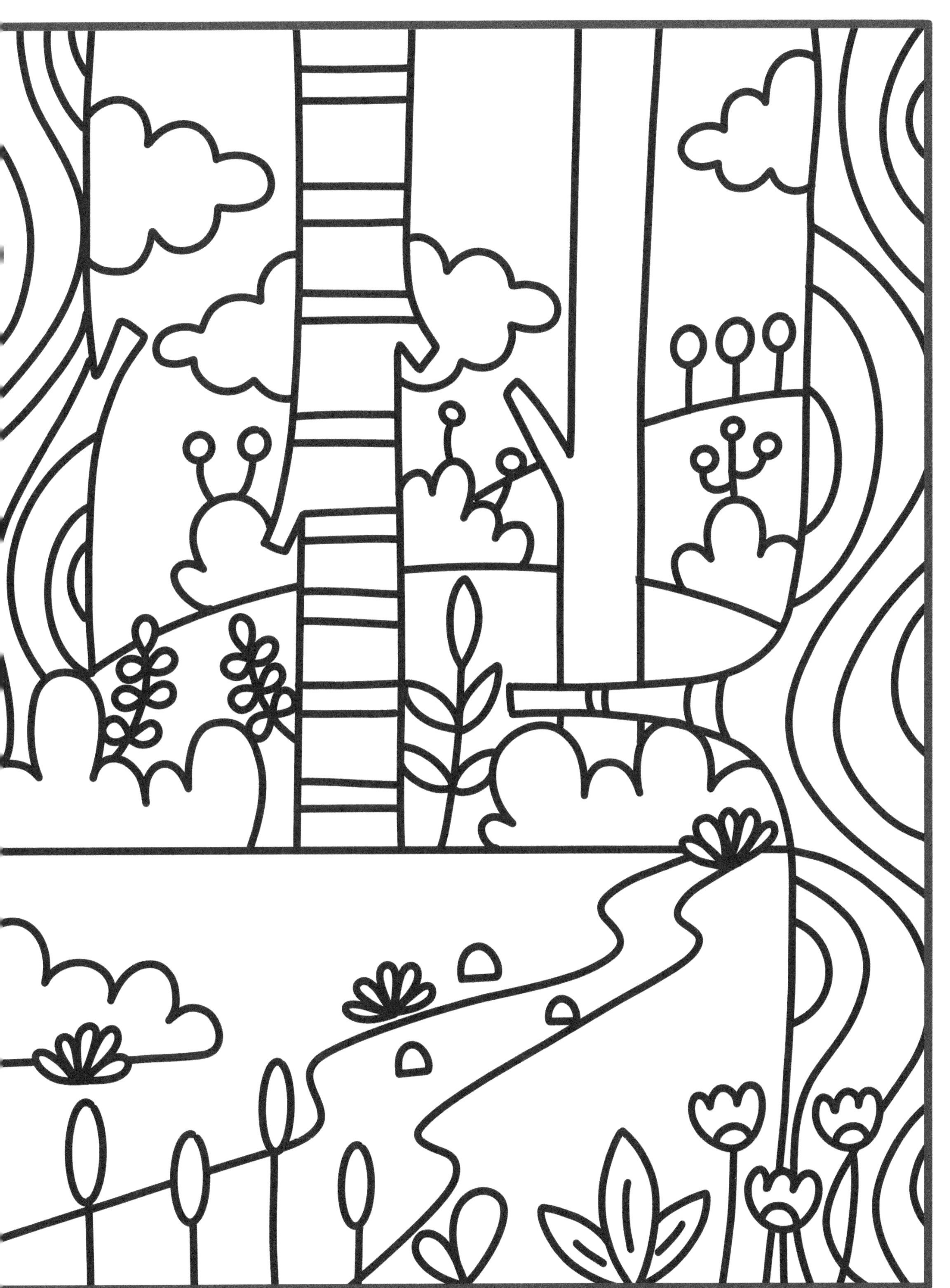

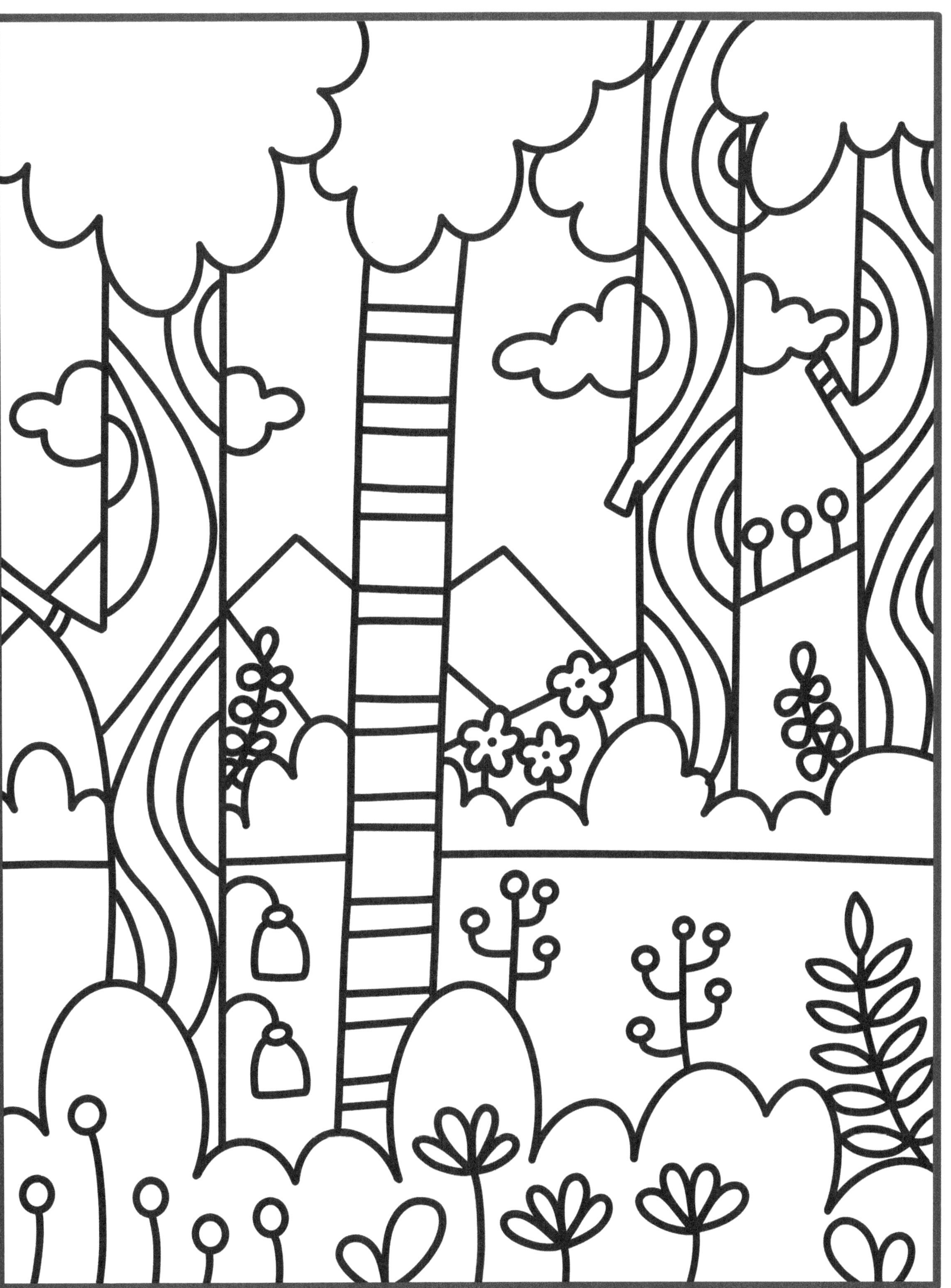

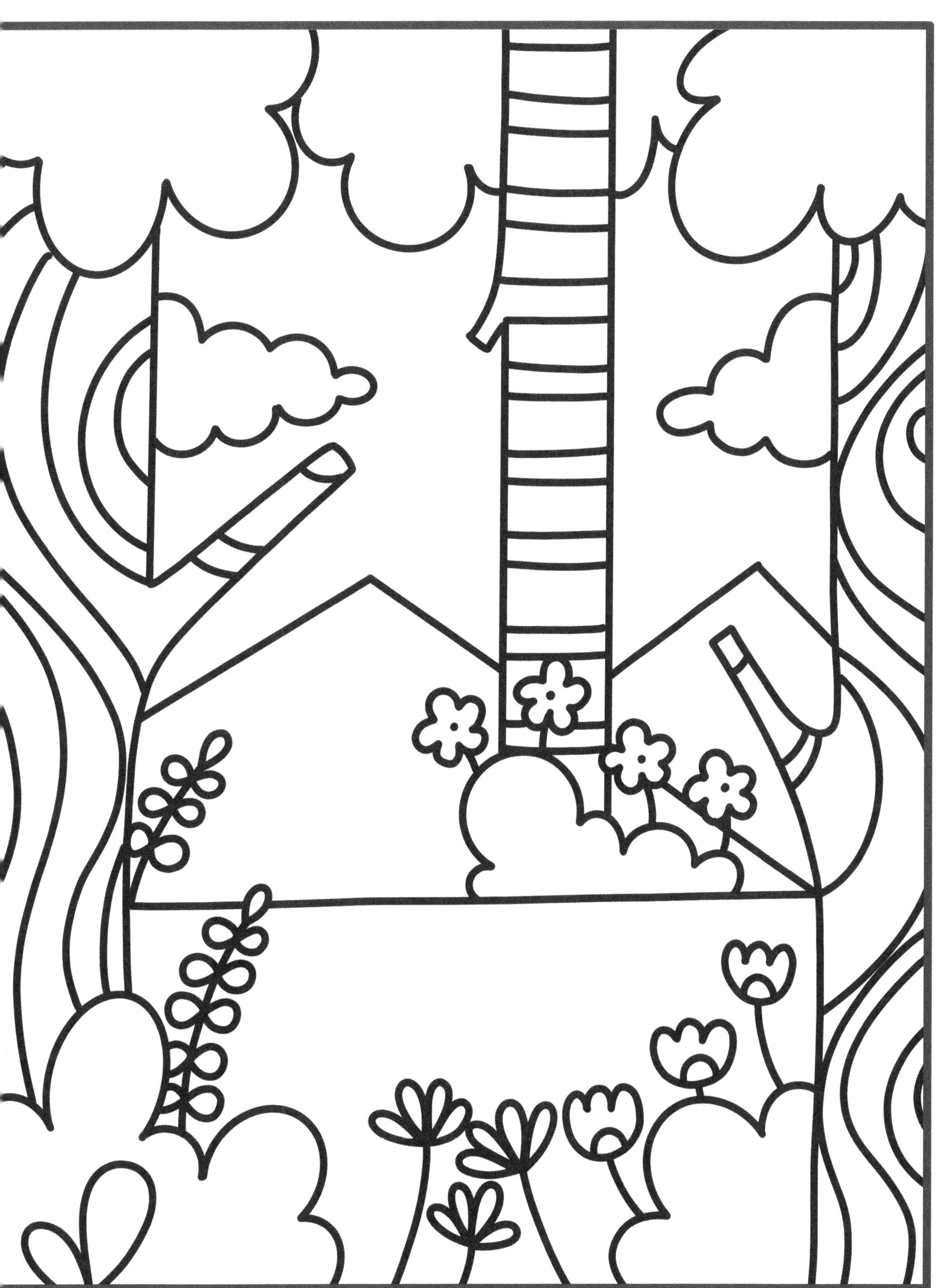

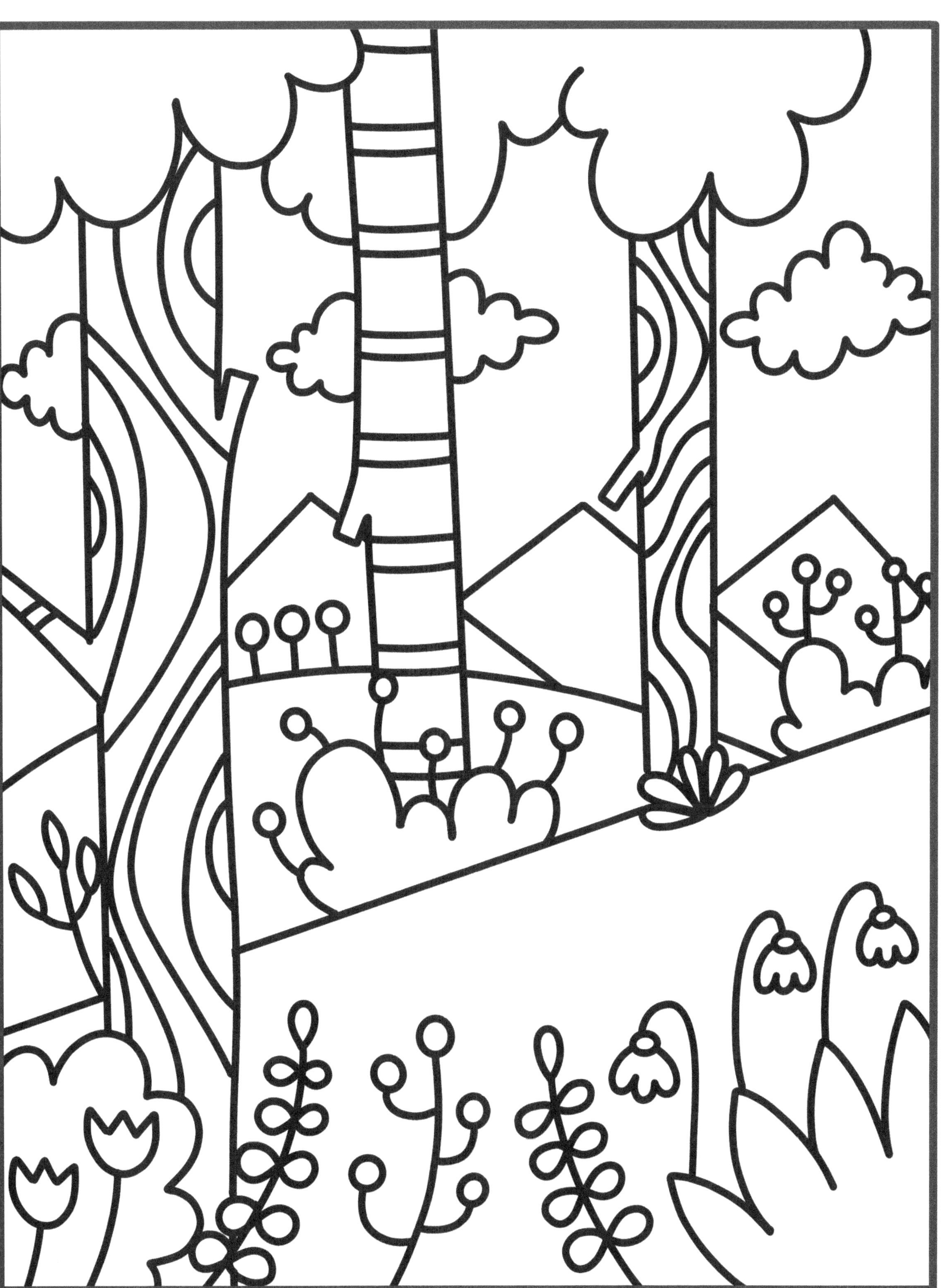

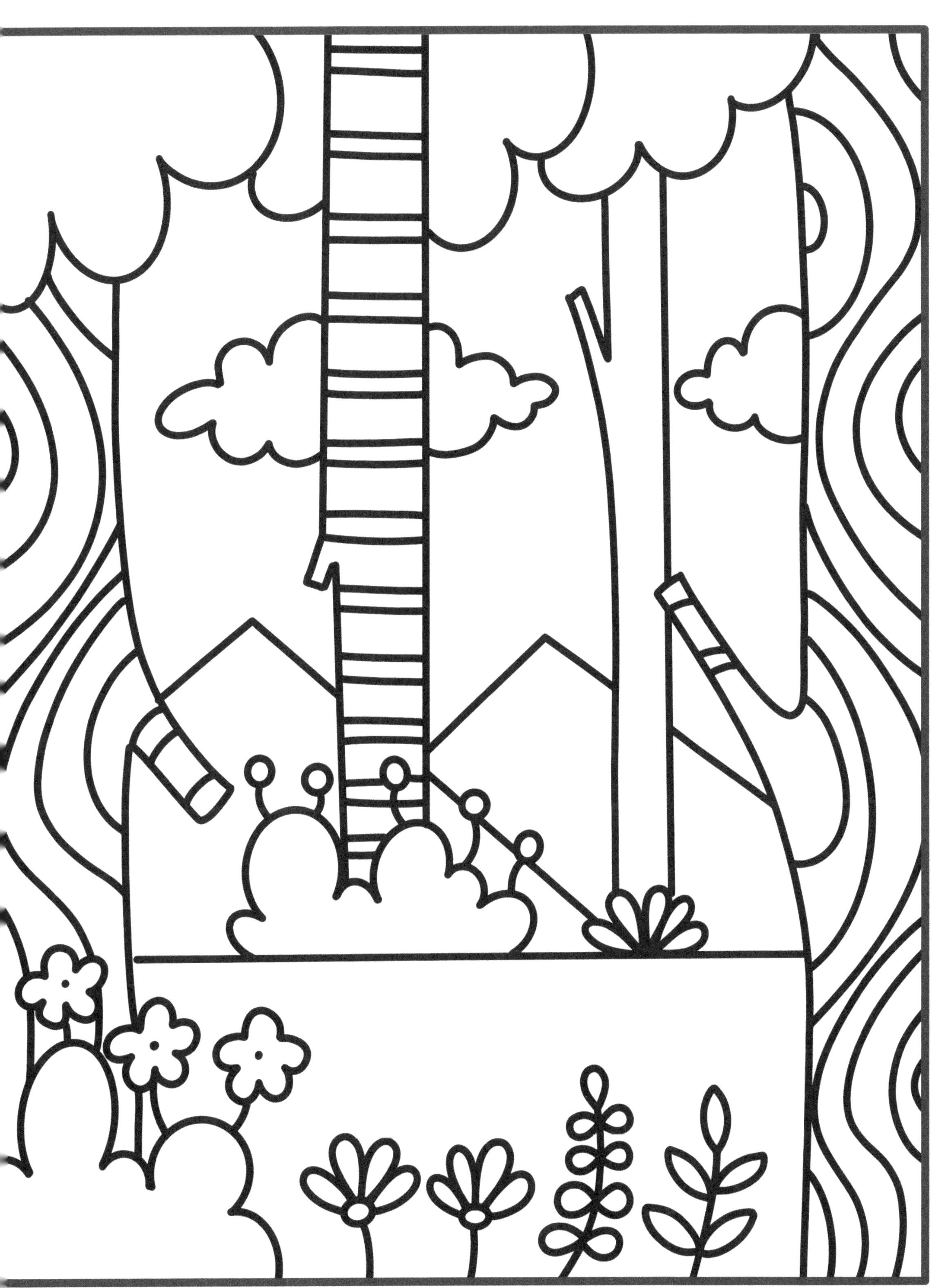

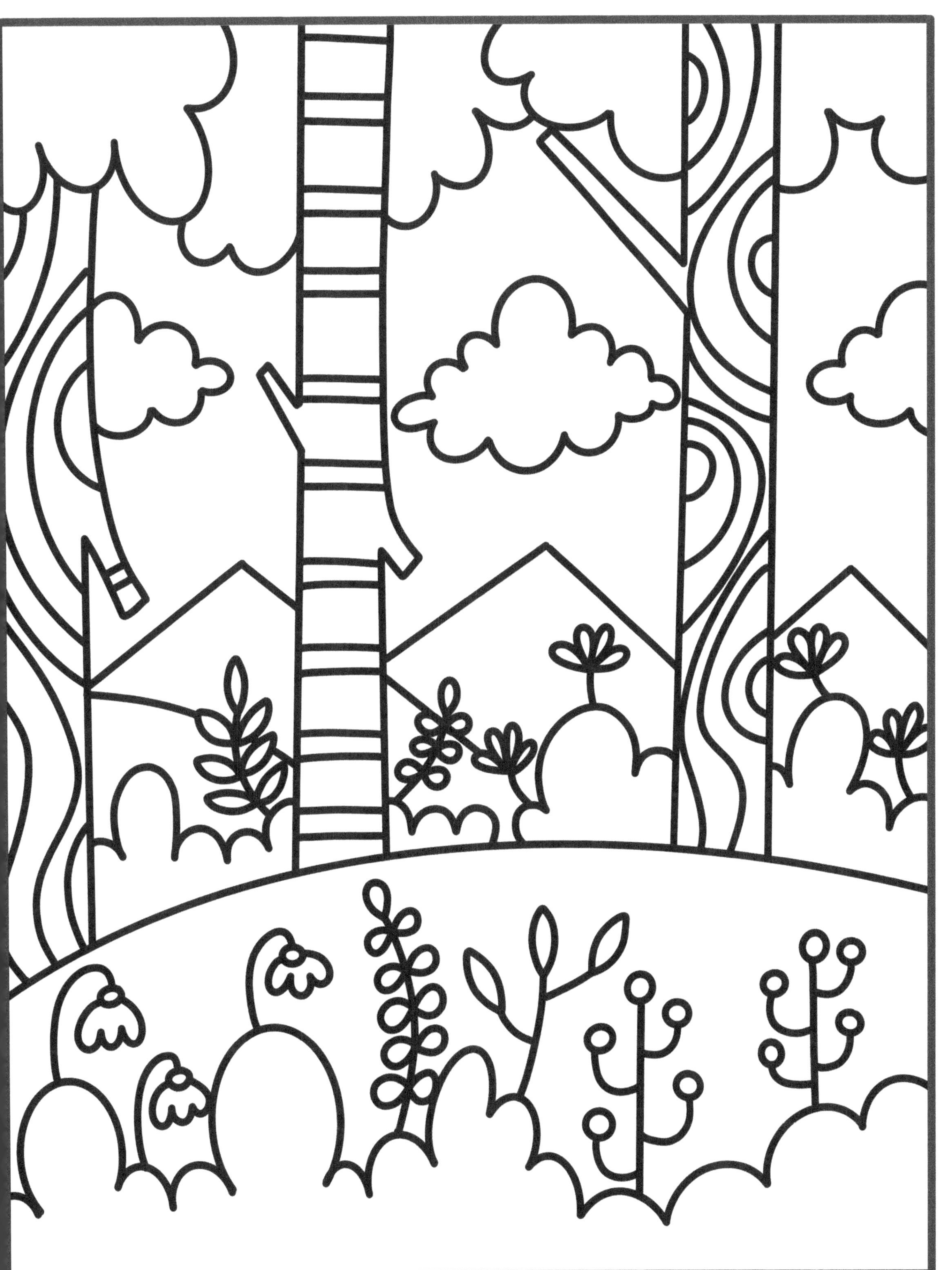

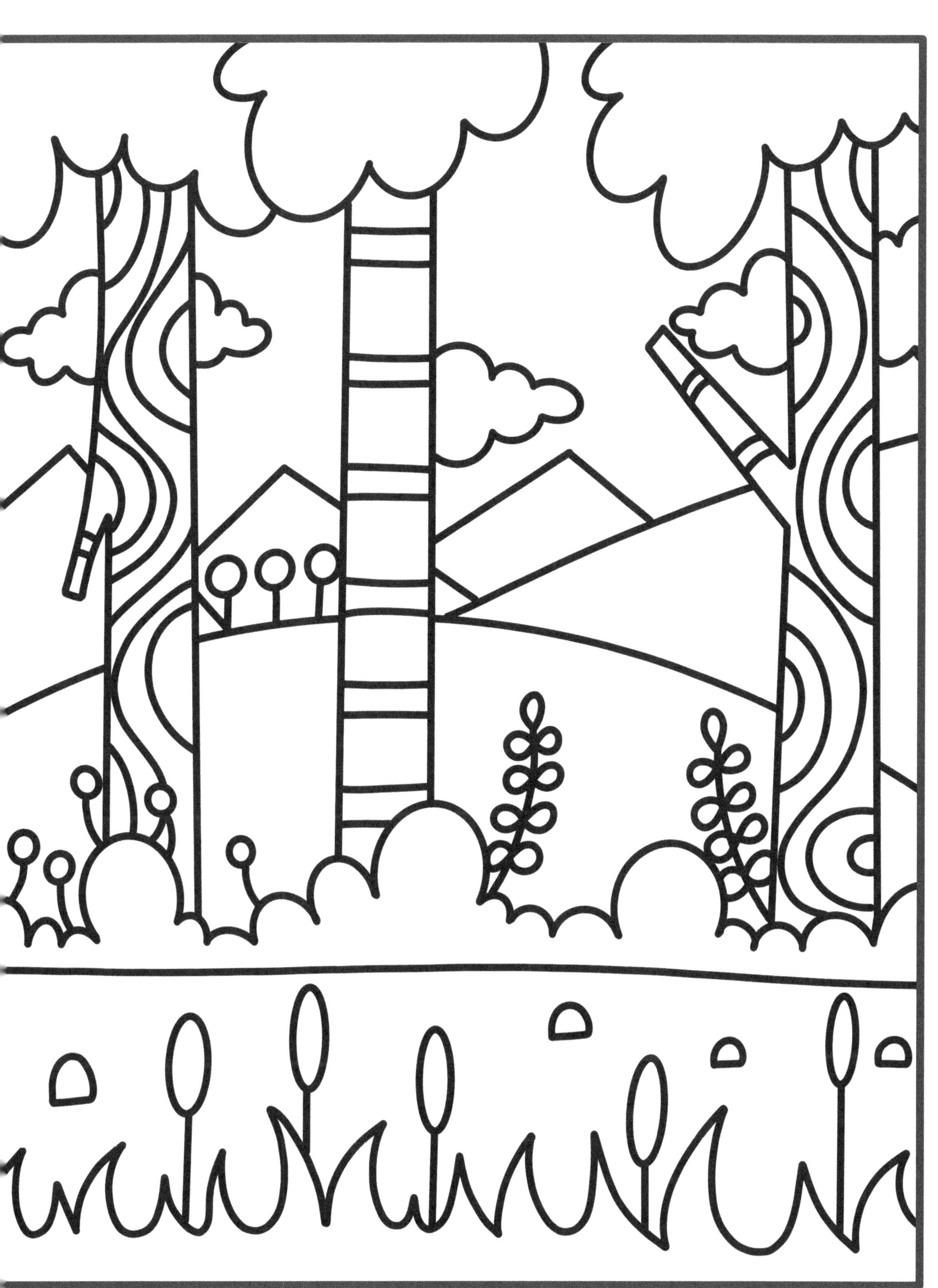

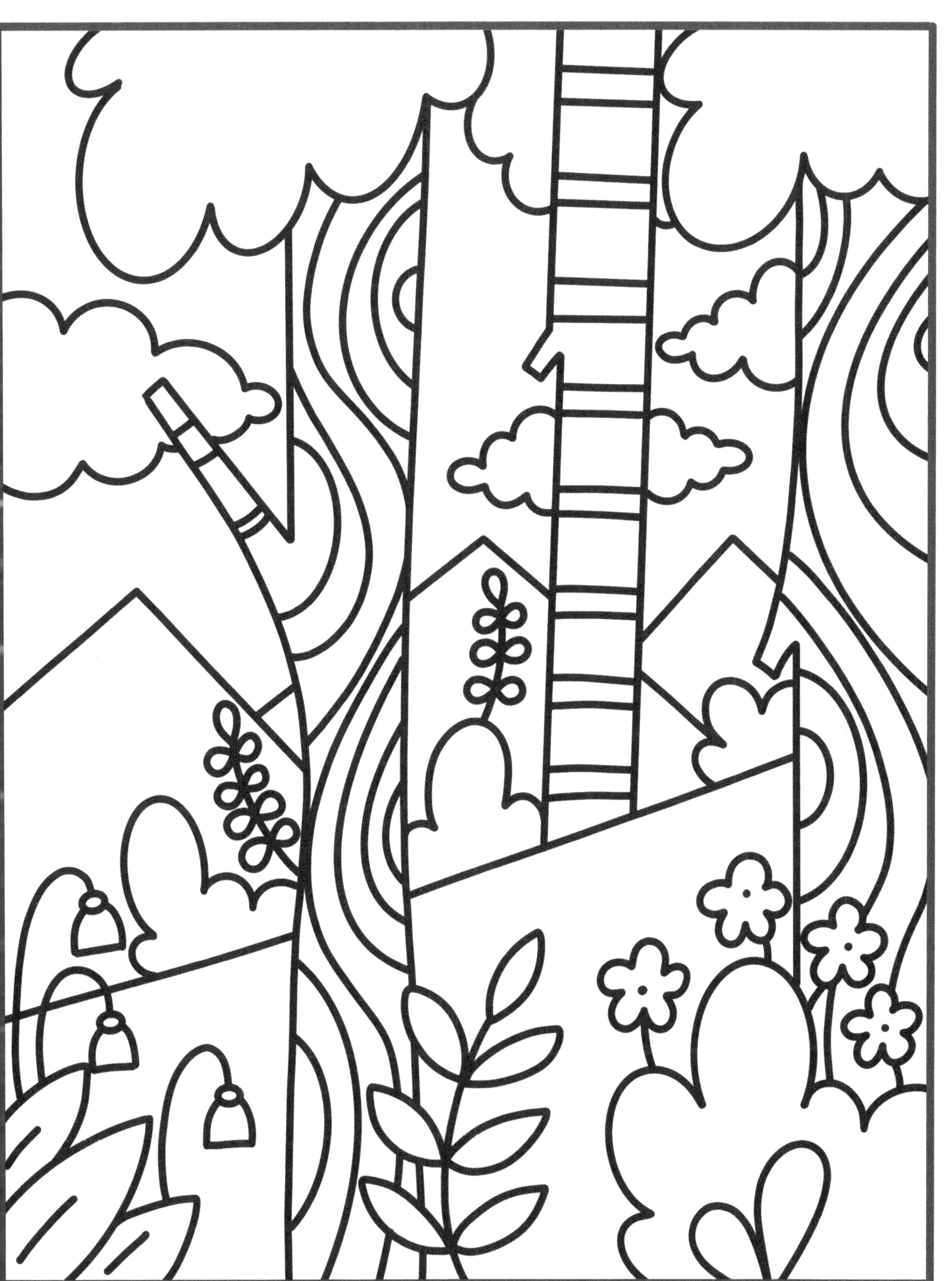

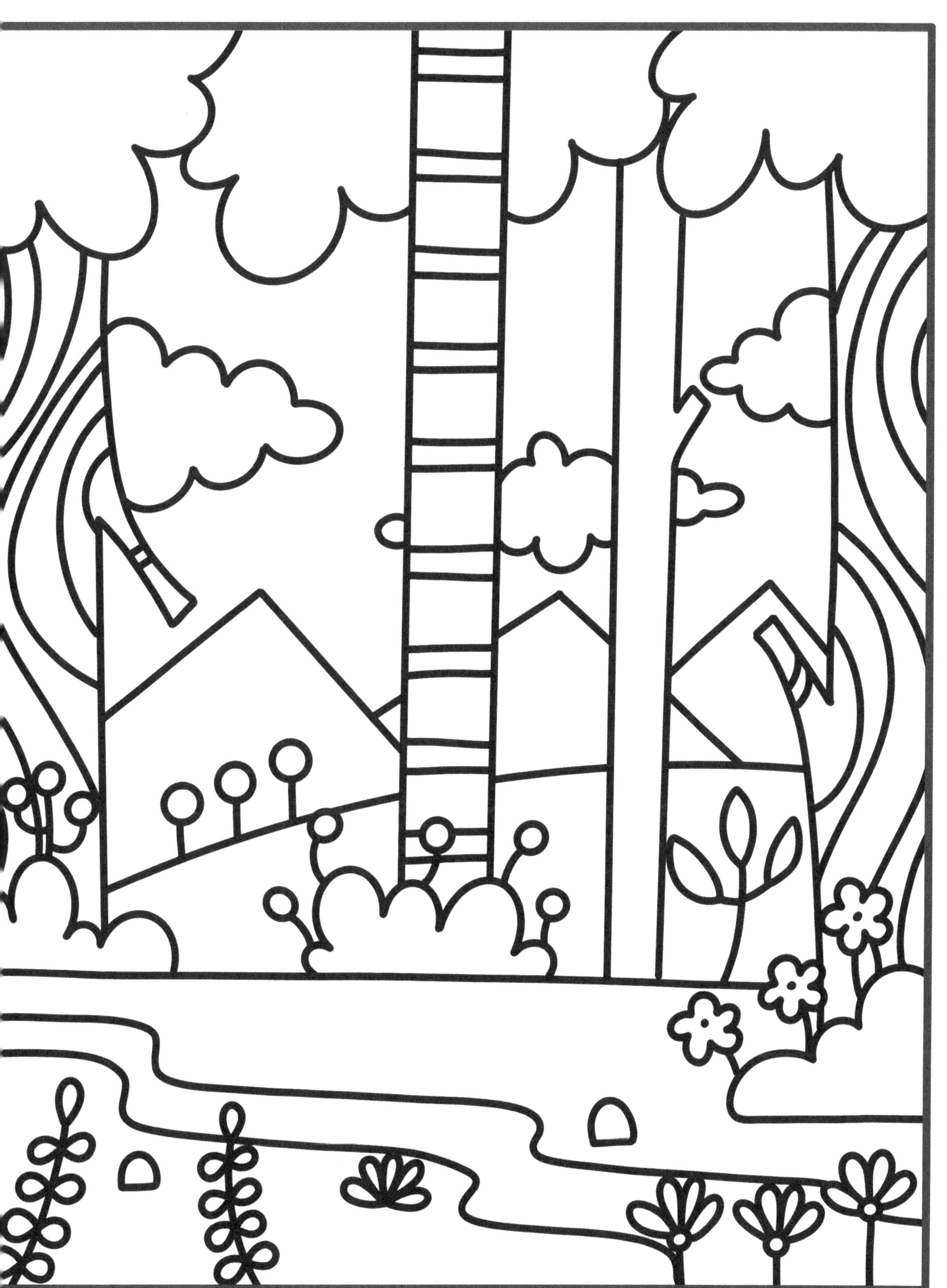

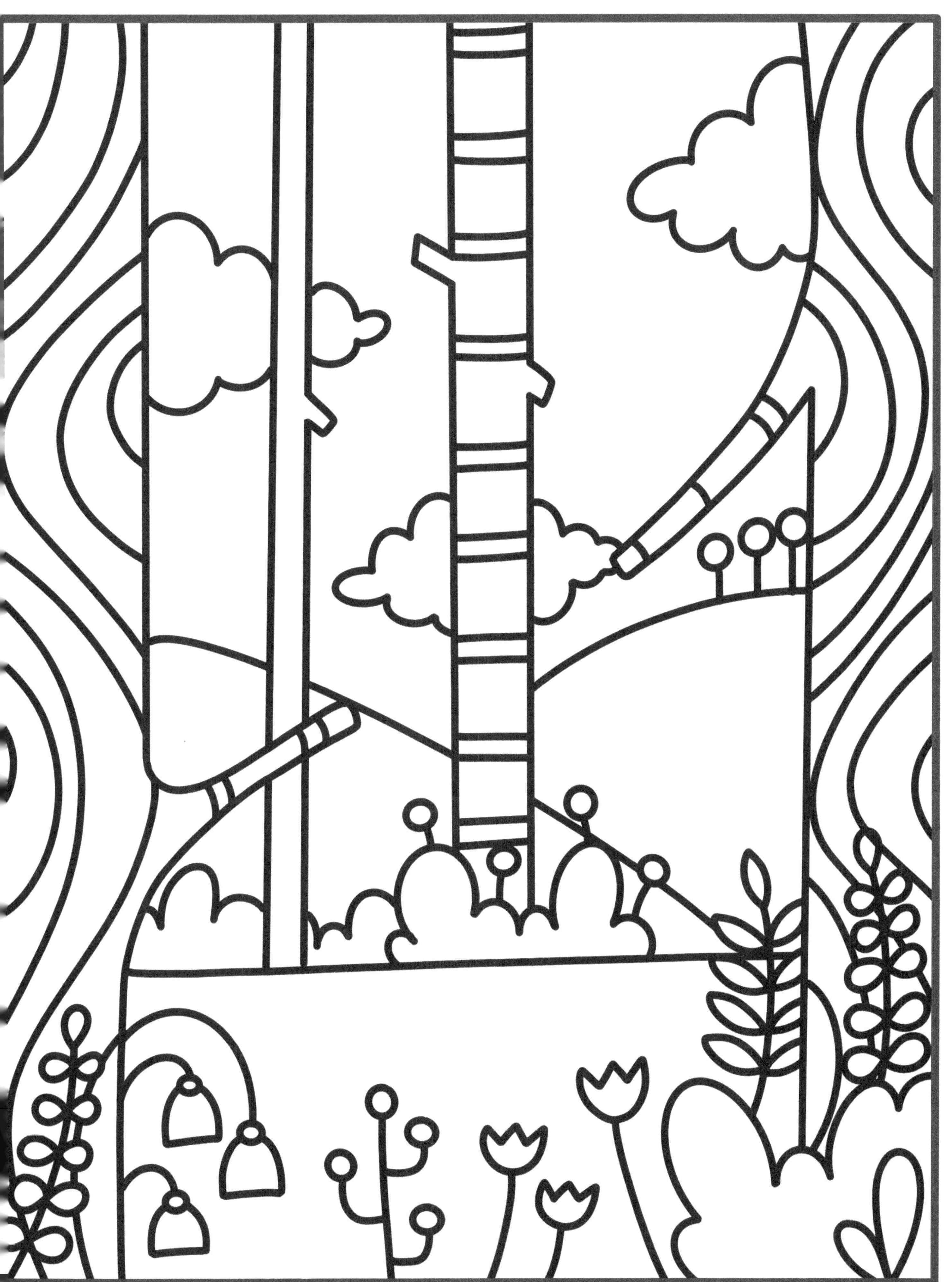